INTRODUCING
ISSUES WITH
OPPOSING
VIEWPOINTS®

Illegal Immigration

INTRODUCING
ISSUES WITH
OPPOSING
VIEWPOINTS®

Illegal Immigration

Sheri Metzger Karmiol, *Book Editor*

Christine Nasso, *Publisher*
Elizabeth Des Chenes, *Managing Editor*

GREENHAVEN PRESS
An imprint of Thomson Gale, a part of The Thomson Corporation

THOMSON
™
GALE

Detroit • New York • San Francisco • New Haven, Conn. • Waterville, Maine • London

© 2007 Thomson Gale, a part of The Thomson Corporation.

Thomson and Star Logo are trademarks and Gale and Greenhaven Press are registered trademarks used herein under license.

For more information, contact
Greenhaven Press
27500 Drake Rd.
Farmington Hills, MI 48331-3535
Or you can visit our Internet site at http://www.gale.com

LIBRARY OF CONGRESS CATALOGING-IN-PUBLICATION DATA

Illegal immigration / Sheri Metzger Karmiol, book editor.
   p. cm. — (Introducing issues with opposing viewpoints)
  Includes bibliographical references and index.
  ISBN-13: 978-0-7377-3573-4 (hardcover)
  1. Illegal aliens--United States. 2. United States--Emigration and immigration—Government policy. I. Karmiol, Sheri Metzger.
  JV6483.I523 2007
  325.73--dc22
                                                      2007005474

ISBN-10: 0-7377-3573-2

Printed in the United States of America

Contents

Foreword

Indulging in a wide spectrum of ideas, beliefs, and perspectives is a critical cornerstone of democracy. After all, it is often debates over differences of opinion, such as whether to legalize abortion, how to treat prisoners, or when to enact the death penalty, that shape our society and drive it forward. Such diversity of thought is frequently regarded as the hallmark of a healthy and civilized culture. As the Reverend Clifford Schutjer of the First Congregational Church in Mansfield, Ohio, declared in a 2001 sermon, "Surrounding oneself with only like-minded people, restricting what we listen to or read only to what we find agreeable is irresponsible. Refusing to entertain doubts once we make up our minds is a subtle but deadly form of arrogance." With this advice in mind, Introducing Issues with Opposing Viewpoints books aim to open readers' minds to the critically divergent views that comprise our world's most important debates.

Introducing Issues with Opposing Viewpoints simplifies for students the enormous and often overwhelming mass of material now available via print and electronic media. Collected in every volume is an array of opinions that captures the essence of a particular controversy or topic. Introducing Issues with Opposing Viewpoints books embody the spirit of nineteenth-century journalist Charles A. Dana's axiom: "Fight for your opinions, but do not believe that they contain the whole truth, or the only truth." Absorbing such contrasting opinions teaches students to analyze the strength of an argument and compare it to its opposition. From this process readers can inform and strengthen their own opinions, or be exposed to new information that will change their minds. Introducing Issues with Opposing Viewpoints is a mosaic of different voices. The authors are statesmen, pundits, academics, journalists, corporations, and ordinary people who have felt compelled to share their experiences and ideas in a public forum. Their words have been collected from newspapers, journals, books, speeches, interviews, and the Internet, the fastest growing body of opinionated material in the world.

Introducing Issues with Opposing Viewpoints shares many of the well-known features of its critically acclaimed parent series, Opposing Viewpoints. The articles are presented in a pro/con format, allowing readers to absorb divergent perspectives side by side. Active reading questions preface each viewpoint, requiring the student to approach the material thoughtfully and carefully. Useful charts, graphs, and cartoons supplement each article. A thorough introduction provides readers with crucial background on an issue. An annotated bibliography points the reader toward articles, books, and Web sites that contain additional information on the topic. An appendix of organizations to contact contains a wide variety of charities, nonprofit organizations, political groups, and private enterprises that each hold a position on the issue at hand. Finally, a comprehensive index allows readers to locate content quickly and efficiently.

Introducing Issues with Opposing Viewpoints is also significantly different from Opposing Viewpoints. As the series title implies, its presentation will help introduce students to the concept of opposing viewpoints, and learn to use this material to aid in critical writing and debate. The series' four-color, accessible format makes the books attractive and inviting to readers of all levels. In addition, each viewpoint has been carefully edited to maximize a reader's understanding of the content. Short but thorough viewpoints capture the essence of an argument. A substantial, thought-provoking essay question placed at the end of each viewpoint asks the student to further investigate the issues raised in the viewpoint, compare and contrast two authors' arguments, or consider how one might go about forming an opinion on the topic at hand. Each viewpoint contains sidebars that include at-a-glance information and handy statistics. A Facts About section located in the back of the book further supplies students with relevant facts and figures.

Following in the tradition of the Opposing Viewpoints series, Greenhaven Press continues to provide readers with invaluable exposure to the controversial issues that shape our world. As John Stuart Mill once wrote: "The only way in which a human being can make some approach to knowing the whole of a subject is by hearing what can be said about it by persons of every variety of opinion and studying all modes in which it can be looked at by every character of mind. No wise man ever acquired his wisdom in any mode but this." It is to this principle that Introducing Issues with Opposing Viewpoints books are dedicated.

Introduction

"For almost a century after the Constitution was adopted, illegal immigration was virtually impossible."[1]

Quite simply, illegal immigration is the entry of non–U.S. citizens into the United States without their having applied for entry at one of the many border crossings from Canada and Mexico or formal customs entry locations, most of which are at airports. While some foreigners enter the United States illegally through international shipping, smuggled into the country among the goods that are unloaded daily, that is not the most common mode of entry. Most illegal immigrants enter through the southern border with Mexico, and as a result, most of the emphasis that has been placed on stemming illegal immigration has focused on how to make the southern border more secure. To understand how the United States went from a country that initially welcomed immigrants to a country of quotas and legal sanctions, it is necessary to examine how immigration has changed to respond to social and cultural ideology.

From Immigrants to Criminals

Illegal immigration is a topic that has become particularly politicized in the past several years, but immigration never used to be illegal at all. In fact, for 230 years, beginning in 1655, all immigrants entered the country by crossing the borders with Canada or Mexico or through our nation's many ports, where they simply disembarked from their ships, found housing, and began their new lives. Initially there was no real effort to impede immigration, and in fact, immigrants were needed to help the country grow and prosper. The United States promoted itself as a country of immigrants and welcomed most of the immigrants who sought to create a new life in a country with seemingly unlimited opportunities. However, after the Revolutionary War the new country felt a need to regulate some of

[1] Samuel P. Huntington, *Who Are We? The Challenges to America's National Identity.* New York: Simon & Schuster, 2004, p. 225.

the immigration that was occurring. In 1790 the new U.S. Congress passed the first immigration law, which required a two-year residency before qualifying for citizenship. In 1795 the residency rule was extended to five years, but by 1798 immigrants needed to be residents for fourteen years. The fourteen-year residency requirement was designed to halt Irish and French immigration, since these refugees had been active in government protests. Within four years, though, the law requiring fourteen years for residency was repealed, and immigration continued as it had previously with little interruption for most of the next sixty years.

By the mid-nineteenth century the rules began to change with the first new laws in 1862, 1875, and 1882 that restricted immigrants from China. Convicts, lunatics, idiots, and those unable to take care of themselves were also excluded from entry. By the end of the nineteenth century, a flood of new immigrants was entering through Ellis Island and similar sites along the eastern part of the United States and the Gulf coast. Most of these immigrants were permitted to seek entry if they were judged capable of work and of supporting themselves and if they did not exhibit evidence of one of the prohibited diseases. In 1891 the Office of Immigration was created and in 1907 those who were determined to be imbeciles, feeble-minded, suffering from tuberculosis, or persons with a physical or mental defect were denied legal entry. In the meantime, the first border patrol agents, called Mounted Inspectors, had been organized in 1904 and had begun patrolling the border between the United States and Mexico, even as new laws were sought to further restrict immigration. An anti-Catholic backlash directed at the many new immigrants coming to the United States from Italy and economic concerns about the arrival of large numbers of poor Jewish peasants from eastern Europe led to increased pressure to reform immigration policy. Eventually literacy tests were imposed, and in 1921 emergency legislation created a tough quota system to bring immigration to a halt.

In 1924 Congress passed the Labor Appropriation Act that established the U.S. Border Patrol as a way to stop illegal entry into the United States. Over the next seventy-five years a succession of changes to immigration laws raised and lowered quotas, removed quotas based on race, and occasionally, as with the 1986 law, even offered illegal immigrants amnesty. Some of these laws, such as the

1948 Displaced Persons Act and the 1953 Refugee Act, were passed in response to the devastation brought by wars, while others, such as the Immigration and Nationality Act of 1952, eliminated earlier laws that had barred immigrants from Asian countries.

Immigration Today

In 1990 Congress passed an immigration law that would set a ceiling of 675,000 immigrants admitted to the United States per year. Illegal immigration, however, still continued with no relief, and so in an effort to deal with the increasing number of illegal immigrants, Congress passed new legislation. The 1996 Illegal Immigration Reform and Immigrant Responsibility Act made it easier to deport illegal immigrants. Even minor offenses such as shoplifting, which might carry only probation and not jail time, could result in deportation. Additionally, any illegal immigrant who lied and claimed to be a U.S. citizen would be barred from ever holding U.S. citizenship. Illegal immigrants who married American citizens or who have American-born children would also be deported under this legislation if any of the provisions of the 1996 law were violated.

Throughout the many years of changing immigration law and imposed quotas, laws such as the one passed in 1996 had little actual effect in halting illegal immigration. After the terrorist attacks of September 2001, however, demands that government solve the problem of illegal immigration increased. In the past few years there have been several proposals to solve the illegal immigration problem, although no new legislation has been passed. What has become clear from recent debate is that illegal immigration is a complex problem that is not easily solved. It has been estimated that there are between 11.5 and 12 million illegal immigrants currently living in the United States. In the following pages of *Introducing Issues with Opposing Viewpoints: Illegal Immigration*, readers will have the opportunity to assess the arguments surrounding this contentious topic.

Chapter 1

Does Illegal Immigration Benefit or Harm American Society?

In addition to the many people who enter the country illegally every year, others still follow the legal process by registering with the government to gain entry.

Viewpoint

1

Illegal Immigrants Positively Impact American Life

"In 2003 alone the labor of undocumented workers poured $7 billion in taxes into Social Security."

Derrick Z. Jackson

Derrick Z. Jackson is an award-winning journalist for the *Boston Globe*, where he has been a columnist since 1988. He was a Nieman Fellow in Journalism at Harvard University in 1984 and a finalist for the Pulitzer Prize for Commentary in 2001. In this op-ed column for the *Boston Globe*, Jackson argues that undocumented workers pay taxes and contribute to the American economy, even though they are often denied access to many government benefits.

AS YOU READ, CONSIDER THE FOLLOWING QUESTIONS:

1. According to the data presented in this viewpoint, in what ways do undocumented immigrants become a part of the American economy?
2. What is the difference in income between legal immigrant families and illegal immigrant families, according to Lipman?

2. What does Standard & Poor's suggest be done with the money that illegal immigrants put into Social Security each year?

At a 2006 New York rally for legalization of immigrants, Chung-Wha Hong, the executive director of the New York Immigration Coalition, said, "We are inseparable, indivisible, and impossible to take out of America." In Phoenix, Victor Colex, a 37-year-old fence builder who makes between $7 and $8 an hour, told the *Washington Post*, "We are not asking for favors. We only want to work, for our families and parents and children." In Boston, 26-year-old Robin Martini, a legal immigrant from Guatemala, told the *Globe*, "We give a grain a day of ourselves to this country. We want to be part of it. We respect the laws. We pay our taxes. We want a piece of the American dream.

Should Illegal Immigrants Be Able to Apply for Legal Status?

The majority of adults in New Jersey believe that illegal immigrants who have lived and worked in the United States for at least two years should keep their jobs.

They should be given a chance to keep their jobs and eventually apply for legal status.

They should be deported back to their native country.

32%

65%

Source: *Boston Globe.*

Americans seem to get this, in a conflicted way. A new *Washington Post*-ABC News poll says that 63 percent of Americans now support legalization of immigrants who have lived here for a certain number of years. A new CBS News poll found that 74 percent of Americans favor letting illegal immigrants who have been in the country at least five years stay and work in the United States providing they pay a fine, pay any back taxes they owe, speak English, and have no criminal record.

The conflicted nature of the acceptance comes in other poll findings that show that Americans still believe that immigrants are a major drain on national resources. A *Time* magazine poll found that 84 percent of Americans were "very" concerned (61 percent) or "somewhat" concerned (23 percent) that it costs taxpayers too much to provide healthcare and education to immigrants. A *Fox News/ Opinion Dynamics* poll last week found that 87 percent of Americans say they are concerned that immigrants "overburden government services and programs."

Illegal Workers Contribute to Social Security

But the evidence is becoming clear that it is justified that immigrants give us more than a grain a day. They give their dollars. They are an inseparable and indivisible part of the economy. In articles published in *The Tax Lawyer*, a publication of the American Bar Association, and in the upcoming issue of the *Harvard Latino Law Review*, Francine Lipman, a professor at Chapman University's law school in Orange, Calif., writes that the widespread belief that undocumented immigrants cost us more than they give us is "demonstrably false." In her review article, Lipman wrote that there are 7 million undocumented workers, which is 1 out of every 20 in the United States. Such undocumented workers live in households where the average annual income is $27,400, compared with nearly $48,000 for legal immigrant families.

They cannot access or easily access many public services, yet in 2003 alone the labor of undocumented workers poured $7 billion in

FAST FACT

According to a Pew Hispanic Center report, the undocumented immigrant population had reached nearly 12 million by March 2006.

Polls show that most Americans favor legalization of immigrants who have lived and worked in the country for at least five years.

taxes into Social Security even though they cannot legally claim those benefits. Lipman calls this "an abyss in federal relief for hard-working, poor families. Undocumented working poor families have higher effective income tax rates than their neighbors who enjoy higher income levels."

They perform jobs that are inseparable from our standard of living. Undocumented workers are about 5 percent of our overall labor force but according to the Pew Hispanic Center's analysis of Census data are between 22 and 36 percent of America's insulation workers, miscellaneous agricultural workers, meat-processing workers, construction workers, dishwashers, and maids. The American Farm Bureau, the lobbying group for agricultural interests, says that without guest workers, the United States would lose $5 billion to $9 billion a year in fruit, vegetable, and flower production and up to 20 percent of production would go overseas.

Illegal Workers Also Pay Taxes

Often ignored by anti-immigration forces is that undocumented workers pay sales taxes and real estate taxes directly if they are home-owners, indirectly if they are renters. Analysts at Standard & Poor's wrote last week that there is no clear correlation between undocumented families and local costs, as the states with the highest numbers of such families also have relatively low unemployment rates, high property values, and strong income growth, "all of which contribute to stable financial performance."

Except, of course, for the undocumented families themselves. Standard & Poor's wrote that the least we could consider in this debate is to redistribute the $7 billion contributed by undocumented workers into Social Security. It said, for instance, that the money could go toward the estimated $11.2 billion it takes to educate the nation's 1.8 million undocumented children. Better still is to take the people who give us a grain a day in the shadows and let them flower in the sunlight of legalization.

EVALUATING THE AUTHOR'S ARGUMENT:

Jackson cites polls showing support for the legalization of illegal immigrants who have lived in this country for a certain period of time. Assuming that you agree with the majority of Americans, how long do you think illegal immigrants should live in the United States before they are given amnesty and citizenship?

Illegal Immigrants Negatively Impact American Life

"Illegal immigrants take food from the refrigerators and clothes from closets."

Stevan Pearce

Congressman Stevan Pearce represents the southern district of New Mexico. In his congressional testimony Pearce explains that illegal immigration is putting the residents of southern New Mexico at risk because of the increase of criminal activity associated with people who cross the border illegally. Pearce explains that illegal immigrants commit crimes and are themselves the victims of crimes. This criminal activity creates an unfair burden on both law enforcement and the judicial system of southern New Mexico.

AS YOU READ, CONSIDER THE FOLLOWING QUESTIONS:

1. According to Pearce, what is the geographical situation that is creating so many problems with illegal immigration in southern New Mexico?

Stevan Pearce, "Impact of Illegal Immigration," FDCH congressional testimony, November 10, 2005.

2. What kinds of criminal activity are being blamed on illegal immigrants crossing into southern New Mexico, according to the author?
3. What kinds of drug activities does Pearce claim are being blamed on illegal immigrants?

The entire U.S. border with Mexico in the State of New Mexico is in my congressional district. It spans 180 miles of mostly open border. . . . For the most part . . . the border contains no barrier whatsoever. Three counties—Hidalgo, Luna and Dona Ana—lie directly on the U.S.-Mexico border, providing 10,000 square miles for circumventing Border Patrol authorities. With approximately 80 agents per shift patrolling this area, there is only 1 agent per every 125 square miles.

This expansive border area has become the conduit of choice for illegal activity over the past two years, due to what I believe is a part of the Border Patrol's flawed national strategy of increasing attention on some areas of the border while failing to recognize the shifting traffic patterns to other areas. In 2004, Customs and Border Protection (CBP) launched the $10 million Arizona Border Control Initiative (ABCI) deploying 260 temporary and permanent Border Patrol agents, unmanned aerial vehicles, Immigration and Customs Enforcement Air and Marine aircraft and helicopters to Arizona without extending similar enforcement augmentation to New Mexico. Consequently, assigning additional resources along the Arizona border resulted in increasing illegal immigration into New Mexico. . . . My constituents report to me daily the extraordinary numbers of illegal immigrants crossing their property—some up to 500 per day just on one ranch—that the Border Patrol never intercepts. . . .

Impact on Residents

The extent and intensity with which illegal immigration is increasing in my district is placing extraordinary costs and danger on residents in this border area. Vandalism and burglary of residents' homes and property are increasing dramatically. Two weeks ago, a constituent informed me that illegal immigrants broke into three houses in Hidalgo County the day before. . . . One of my constituents has been burglarized by illegal immigrants three times in the past two years. The illegal immigrants take food from the refrigerators and clothes from closets. Constituents often inform me that their trucks, cars and tractors are stolen and used to escape from Border Patrol. In August, I was informed that human smugglers stole a school bus from the school bus facility in Lordsburg.

There are many sections where the fence at the U.S.-Mexico border has not been completed, as seen here in Jacumba, California.

It is not only private residences that have been burglarized, but businesses in the communities close to the border. Due to the lack of detention bed space, the Border Patrol stations in my district have been forced to release apprehended illegal immigrants into our communities, such as the parking lots of the local McDonalds and Wal-Mart. Shortly after, the police departments receive calls that the Family Dollar Store and other businesses in the community have been burglarized.

Many of the residents live on ranches on the U.S.-Mexico border, where there is no fence or barrier. These ranchers have built their own barbed wire fences to keep their cattle from entering Mexico. However, the fences are routinely destroyed, often by human and drug smugglers driving directly over the fences. Earlier this year, a 1.1 mile section of a rancher's border fence was stolen, leaving the border wide open for his cattle to be lost completely. Despite the fact that the fence is on a 60 ft. government right [of way] that runs along the border, the Federal government will not reimburse the ranchers for the destruction of the fence. The ranchers rebuilt the 1.1 mile fence at their own cost of $5,000. Yet, the fence is continually broken, costing the ranchers $250 per day to maintain it. Other ranchers inform me that the solar windmills that power water generation for their cattle are constantly damaged costing $800 per windmill to repair. Furthermore, residents are faced with the daily task of cleaning up the massive amounts of debris left behind by the illegal immigrants, including clothes, food, trash, syringes, human feces—enough to fill several tractor trailers . . . in the words of one of my constituents.

Bandit activity is the latest disturbingly growing trend threatening the lives of residents along the border. The human smugglers are partnering with Mexican bandits, who are robbing the illegal immigrants as the smugglers bring them across the border. Competing bandits are beginning to fight over the groups of smuggled immigrants even on the U.S. side. One of the ranchers and her daughter—while checking their border fence for damage on horseback

—recently rode upon a bandit shoot out. Thankfully, they were not injured, this time.

The bandit activity has become so prevalent that the Border Patrol has even warned residents not to go near their own border fences. It is patently offensive when the government agency responsible for protecting the residents warns them not to go repair their own border fence—a fence the Federal government refuses to maintain —because the Border Patrol cannot effectively gain control of the border.

Impact on Local Law Enforcement Agencies

Due to the expansive nature of my district's border area, and limited border security resources, local law enforcement agencies have long supplemented the Border Patrol in responding to and apprehending unlawful entries and illegal immigrants committing criminal offenses. However, the extent and intensity with which illegal activity is increasing is extracting a costly and dangerous toll on local law enforcement agencies not only in border communities, but communities throughout the district.

Police and sheriff departments are increasingly called on a daily basis to respond to large groups of illegal immigrants hiding in fields or to intercept car and truck loads of illegal immigrants on behalf of the Border Patrol. The groups have become so large that it is taking an entire shift of officers to respond to, chase and apprehend the illegal immigrants and wait for Border Patrol officers to return from patrolling other areas of the border in order to process the illegal immigrants. It costs the Luna County Sheriff's Department up to $800 each time they respond to such instances. Law enforcement agencies in border communities across the district tell me it requires 25% of their operating budgets to supplement the Border Patrol in this manner.

Another component straining local law enforcement agencies is responding to criminal activity by illegal immigrants. The Luna County Sheriff's Department indicates that criminal offenses by illegal immigrants—including hit and runs, stolen vehicles and domestic violence and drug seizures—have grown to 150 since the beginning of the year alone. The Chief of Police Clare May in Columbus, New Mexico, a village that sits directly on the border,

While deportation of large numbers of undocumented immigrants occurs, there are still many more who remain and can become the victims or perpetrators of crimes.

stated that stolen cars have increased from 5 cars a year in 2003 to almost 20 cars just in one month last year. Routinely, the local law enforcement agencies must intercept the stolen vehicles while full of illegal immigrants, which often result in high speed chases through our small border communities. Several of the high speed pursuits have resulted in rollovers and deaths of the smuggler and the illegal immigrants inside. However, most result in arrests, with discovery of large amounts of marijuana or cocaine. These criminal cases place a massive burden on the local departments particularly because the officers must process the criminals and detain them until they can appear before a judge. Most offensive is the mandate that local law enforcement departments must contact the Mexican consulate and wait for the Mexican government's action to ensure proper representation for the criminals, prolonging the time in which the local departments have had to detain the criminal aliens.

Jails in the border area will typically detain the criminal aliens for up to 6 months at a cost of approximately $50 per day per inmate. Much of this is not reimbursed. Last year, one county applied for $60,000 in State Criminal Alien Assistance Program (SCAAP) funding and received $4,800. While such responses are indeed imposing a burdensome financial cost on the departments, it is severely compromising the safety of residents when officers are pulled away from their normal duties in communities and counties.

Local law enforcement agencies are not only impacted by the extent to which illegal activity has increased, but also the growing intensity of the dangerous activity. The drug and human smugglers' counter intelligence is so sophisticated, and the stakes have become so high for the smugglers, that they are threatening the lives of local law enforcement officers. In early August 2005, the Columbus Police Chief barely escaped a sniper's two gunfire shots while investigating two abandoned cars. Also, Sheriff Deputies have been approached by human and drug smugglers and told the smugglers know who their families are and where they live and they will be killed if the officers get in their way. . . .

The police departments along the border in my district are small, they have small budgets, and their officers work with neither healthcare nor retirement. With it taking 25% of their operating budget, these departments cannot withstand the pressures illegal immigration is putting on their forces. Moreover, supplementing the work of the Border Patrol is compromising local law enforcement departments' primary duty of protecting the citizens of their communities.

Impact on Local Hospitals

The extraordinary costs of the Federal mandate to provide emergency care to illegal immigrants is pushing my district's local hospitals' resources beyond their capacity to cope. Each year, thousands of illegal immigrants require emergency care for heat exhaustion or other severe injuries as they enter New Mexico. Human smugglers leave many of these individuals behind, while others have simply come to the port of entry either sick or in labor.

Mimbres Memorial Hospital in Deming, New Mexico reports that . . . one quarter of all patients treated last year were illegal immigrants. Providing emergency care to illegal immigrants costs the hospital at least $400,000 per month. This does not include the cost to transport the illegal immigrants via helicopter to larger city hospitals, such as El Paso. These rising costs are making it extremely difficult for hospitals to continue operating in my district. When it already takes residents up to an hour to get to the nearest hospital, we cannot afford another hospital leaving our area.

Impact on the Federal Court

Rising levels of illegal immigration continues to break the back of the Federal judiciary in my district as well. Even as we become more successful at securing the border through additional Border Patrol staff and technology, the caseload will continue to burden the United States District Court of New Mexico, specifically the Las Cruces federal courthouse. . . .

Signe Wilkinson Editorial Cartoon © 2006 Signe Wilkinson. All rights reserved. Used permission of Signe Wilkinson and the Washington Post Writers Group in conjunction with the Cartoonist Group. Printed originally in the *Philadelphia Daily News*.

Criminal filings per judgeship in the District are the highest in the nation at 366 per judgeship. The national average is 89. The exceptional caseload is primarily attributed to the geographical factors unique to the District and other border Districts. Immigration and narcotics cases are almost exclusively driving the increase—placing an extraordinary burden on the Las Cruces federal courthouse, which is just 50 miles away from the U.S.-Mexico border. In fact, two-thirds of all criminal cases in the District are now processed in Las Cruces. Immigration prosecutions currently account for 85 percent of all criminal cases in the District. Additionally, the amount of time in which these cases are adjudicated is increasing simultaneously with the caseload as the immigration cases predominantly require interpretation. . . .

Suggestions for Addressing the Urgent Problem

We do not have much more time to secure our border. Frankly, it is not a matter of if, but when, one of my constituents is severely injured or killed due to the unimpeded illegal activity led by dangerous human and drug smugglers. If that happens, it will bring any opportunity for a rational discussion on border security and immigration reform to a grinding halt. . . .

We must commit the Federal resources needed to effectively detect, apprehend and return illegal immigrants—including boots on the ground, technology and the judicial resources. We must commit to the detention bed space needed to end the offensive policy of "catch and release" that only incentivizes illegal immigration. We must also begin to hold the nations from which these illegal immigrants arrive accountable for failure to cooperate with the United States. . . .

In all reality, any border security efforts will be in vain if we fail to simultaneously address the reasons contributing to the flow of illegal immigration into this country. The majority of the illegal immigrants coming here simply want to work. Businesses along the border and elsewhere rely on this labor. Yet there is no effective legal channel for these immigrants to come here to work. Our policies have become even hypocritical—indicating that "we need you to come over and work, but we are going to make it difficult and even deadly for you to do so."

As long as our immigration policies make it difficult to come here to work temporarily on a legal basis, those on both sides—workers and employers—will fill the need illegally. The consequence is a huge flow of illegal immigration to which we must respond, often subtracting from the capability to focus on drug smuggling and terrorists.

EVALUATING THE AUTHOR'S ARGUMENT:

Congressman Pearce argues that illegal immigrants are responsible for a significant increase in criminal activity in southern New Mexico. He does not mention what percentage of illegal immigrants are involved in such activities. Do you find Pearce's argument compelling? If so, what details are most convincing? If you would like more facts to convince you that illegal immigrants are responsible for increases in crime, what additional information should Pearce have supplied?

Illegal Immigrants Create an Economic Benefit for American Businesses

Mary Lou Pickel and Matt Kempner

"Across the nation, four out of five agricultural workers are illegal immigrants and virtually all are Latino."

Mary Lou Pickel and Matt Kempner are staff writers for the *Atlanta Journal-Constitution*. In this article Pickel and Kempner report that illegal immigrants keep labor costs low in agricultural and construction fields and that this helps to keep consumer costs lower. Although some employers claim to verify that the workers they hire are not illegal immigrants, their claim is based on documentation that cannot be verified as authentic, thus allowing these employers to keep wages and the costs of services low.

1. What did Tifton farmer Bill Brim say were the reasons that farmers give for using illegal immigrants?

2. President of Peachtree Homes Hugh Morton states that if immigrants left Georgia, subcontractors might have to double wages. Although he includes both legal and illegal immigrants in his statement, since only illegal workers might be forced to leave the United States, what do Morton's comments really suggest about the number of illegal immigrants working in construction?

3. One large Georgia poultry farmer says that they "don't knowingly hire illegal aliens but we hire a bunch of Mexican people." Since he admits that if he lost these workers there would be no chickens in the grocery store, there is an implication that his workers could be deported and so are illegal. Which of the companies mentioned in this brief article appear to be dishonest in their claims regarding hiring illegal immigrants?

Consider some truths about Georgia's economy: Agriculture is big. Carpet manufacturing is big. Construction, chicken processing, lodging and restaurants are big. And one thick thread ties them all together: reliance on immigrant workers. . . . Many business people say cutting Georgia's immigrant work force . . . would be costly for companies and consumers.

Some Employers Admit They Hire Illegal Workers

While most companies won't admit to using illegal laborers, Tifton farmer Bill Brim makes no bones about having done so in the past. Eliminating those workers would be "an economic disaster" for produce farmers, he said. For years Brim used illegal immigrants to harvest his crops, he said, but now the part-owner of Lewis Taylor Farms uses legal immigrants through a federal contract worker program because

FAST FACT

The 1996 immigration law forced illegal immigrants who wanted a permanent visa to leave the United States before applying.

Do Immigrants Affect Wages?

The estimated number of illegal immigrants in a state's population shows no apparent correlation with the median wage for less-educated workers in that state.

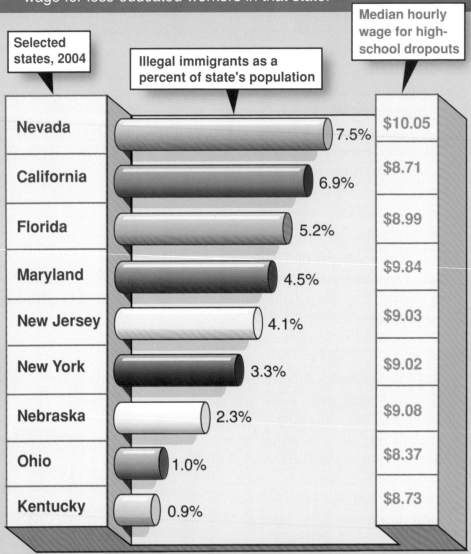

Selected states, 2004	Illegal immigrants as a percent of state's population	Median hourly wage for high-school dropouts
Nevada	7.5%	$10.05
California	6.9%	$8.71
Florida	5.2%	$8.99
Maryland	4.5%	$9.84
New Jersey	4.1%	$9.03
New York	3.3%	$9.02
Nebraska	2.3%	$9.08
Ohio	1.0%	$8.37
Kentucky	0.9%	$8.73

Source: Pew Hispanic Center, Economic Policy Institute analysis of Current Population Survey data.

even illegal immigrants are hard to come by. The federal program is cumbersome, said Brim, who heads the Georgia Fruit & Vegetable Growers Association's immigration committee. In addition to government-set wages, he is required to pay for housing, transportation and other fees. It doubles labor costs compared to what most farmers pay for illegal workers, he said.

Across the nation, four out of five agricultural workers are illegal immigrants and virtually all are Latino, said Demetrios Papademetriou of the Migration Policy Institute, citing a Department of Labor study. Dependence on low-paid illegal immigrants allows Americans to spend less for goods and services, said Papademetriou, president of the Washington think tank that studies the effects of population movement. "Illegal immigration is a subsidy to the way of life here," he said. "It's become a drug." . . .

No Clear Way to Separate Illegal Workers from Legal Workers

Many companies say they comply with federal law and check employees for legal work documents. But some acknowledge the documents could be false, and say it's anybody's guess how much of the work force is illegal.

Georgia is feeling the effects of rapid immigration. The state's foreign-born population grew by 233 percent between 1990 and 2000, according to the Migration Policy Institute. But there are wide-ranging estimates on how many of them are here illegally. One often-quoted source, the Pew Hispanic Center, a nonpartisan research group in Washington, estimates that 350,000 illegal immigrants lived in Georgia in 2004. Nationwide, the number of illegal immigrants is about 12 million, 7.2 million of them workers, the center said. That's roughly 5 percent of the nation's work force. . . .

Hugh Morton, president of Southside builder Peachtree Homes, said if immigrants, including illegal immigrants, were to leave the construction business, subcontractors might have to double current wages of $10 to $12 an hour for semi-skilled work to encourage "college kids to come out and work in the sweat trades." Without immigrant labor, house prices could increase 35 percent, Morton predicted, and the time it takes to build a house could double.

A loss of immigrant laborers also could double the cost of land-scaping services, said Metro Atlanta Landscape and Turf Association executive director Mary Kay Woodworth. "You'd not have as much of a pool of available workers, so you'd have to pay overtime and more benefits and higher wages to attract workers," Woodworth said. The going wage for unskilled landscaping jobs is about $8 per hour.

Likewise, the hotel industry in Georgia has become a magnet for workers from other countries who are willing to take tough, low-paying jobs, such as housekeeping, where starting wages can be $7

An immigrant participates in a rally demonstrating the ways in which immigrant labor supports the American economy.

to $10 an hour. Most hotel owners—particularly those with national chains—make a concerted effort to verify workers are properly documented, said Paul Breslin, the managing partner of a hotel development company and a former manager for three big downtown Atlanta hotels. He suspects that less than 1 percent of the workers in the entire hotel industry in Georgia are here illegally. Still, he said, because his industry is one of Georgia's biggest employers: "One percent is a pretty sizable number of people."

Some Industries Say They Have Zero Illegal Workers

Roy Bowen, president of the Association of Georgia's Textile, Carpet and Consumer Products Manufacturers, said immigrants make up perhaps 20 percent of his industry's labor pool. "As far as we are concerned, everybody who is employed by us is a documented legal worker," said Bowen, whose association includes 65 member companies with about 80,000 employees. For that reason, he said, there would be no impact on his industry if the United States were to remove every illegal worker in the nation.

Summerville attorney Bobby Lee Cook said he finds Bowen's statements amusing. Cook represents American-born former employees of Mohawk Industries who are suing the Calhoun-based carpet maker. They claim Mohawk has knowingly employed a large number of illegal immigrants, thus keeping wages unnaturally low. Mohawk, which didn't respond to requests for comment, has appealed the case to the U.S. Supreme Court, which is scheduled to hear arguments. . . .

The poultry industry also depends on immigrant labor, and two large companies in Georgia—Fieldale Farms and Goldkist—say they ask for documents proving a job candidate is legally allowed to work. They look for a U.S. passport, a green card, a driver's license, Social Security card or other documents accepted under federal law. Goldkist participates in the Department of Homeland Security's pilot program for verifying work papers. Fieldale Farms Chief Financial Officer Tom Hensley said, "If the documents look to be real and legitimate, we hire them." Questioning the validity of the documents could violate the employee's civil rights, he said.

Fieldale pays about $10 an hour to workers who process chickens. About 75 percent of its 4,000 workers in three northeast Georgia chicken-processing plants are immigrants. They are from Vietnam, Laos, Guatemala and Peru—but mostly from Mexico. "We don't knowingly hire illegal aliens, but we hire a bunch of Mexican people, and we love them," Hensley said. "If all the Mexicans were forced to leave tomorrow, there would be no chicken in the grocery store."

EVALUATING THE AUTHORS' ARGUMENT:

Pickel and Kempner note that some companies check for documentation that prove that laborers are not in the United States illegally, but company officials acknowledge that they cannot prove that the documents are valid and that checking their authenticity would be a violation of workers' civil rights. Since forged documents are actually quite common, what additional kinds of proof might employers use to verify that they are hiring legal workers?

Viewpoint

4

"Illegal immigrants don't pay taxes but do consume government services, especially medical care and education."

Illegal Immigrants Create an Economic Disaster for American Businesses

Geoffrey Colvin

Geoffrey Colvin is *Fortune* magazine's senior editor at large. In this essay Colvin argues that illegal immigration is an economic disaster for businesses and government services. In addition, illegal immigrants fail to contribute economically, make a mockery of the American legal system, and make fools of American taxpayers, who must support the influx of illegal immigrants.

AS YOU READ, CONSIDER THE FOLLOWING QUESTIONS:

1. Why, in the author's opinion, are politicians so reluctant to talk about illegal immigration?
2. According to Colvin, there are two reasons why illegal immigration is "big trouble." What are these two reasons?

3. How does the hiring of illegal immigrants lead to lower wages for other people employed in similar jobs, according to Colvin?

Nearly all politicians of all parties would endure the agony of remaining silent for an entire day rather than say a word about one increasingly high-voltage issue: illegal immigrants. . . . There's the problem for politicians, whose first commandment is "exclude no one." Any action against illegal immigrants infuriates a lot of Hispanic voters, whom no one can afford to infuriate. Yet continued inaction is impossible.

Illegal Immigration Has Increased

The main reason is that illegal immigration increased hugely in the '90s. The illegal population is apparently around eight million, increasing by a half million a year. Perversely, a trumpeted toughening of border security may have made matters worse: Border patrols apprehend more people, but more people are trying to cross, so just as many get through as before—but now they stay longer because they know that if they leave the U.S., they might never get back in.

This is big trouble for a couple of reasons, the first being simple economics. Illegal immigrants don't pay taxes but do consume government services, especially medical care and education. By law, these services cannot be denied them. In fact, it's illegal for a hospital even to inquire about a patient's citizenship or immigration status.

In parts of the country with lots of illegal immigrants—the 24 U.S. counties that border Mexico, plus much of the rest of California—the situation is becoming debilitating. Senator Dianne Feinstein of California estimates medical costs for illegal immigrants are running about $1 billion a year in her state; with superb political instincts, she's blaming no one and simply backing a bill to reimburse state and local hospitals with federal

People who oppose letting illegal immigrants stay cite the strain they cause on the economy by not paying taxes to support public services like schools and hospitals.

money. I spoke recently with an administrator of a Texas hospital in a border county, and he says current rules imperil his hospital and drive him nuts. And by the way, he's not allowed to call immigrants illegal. They're undocumented.

The Larger Economic Picture

The full economic effects are much wider. Employers who hire illegals pay them cash and thus evade employment taxes. They may also not report revenue from the work the illegals do and thus evade income taxes. Companies that compete with these employers must cut their own costs, mostly by paying their own workers (regardless of status) lower cash wages under the table, and the tax evasion spreads further.

A downward spiral begins. Government revenues decline while demand for government services goes up. The burden on taxpayers grows heavier. They respond by finding their own ways to avoid taxes or simply by leaving, making the problem even worse. Until recently this was mostly a theoretical worry, but the recent rapid increase in illegal immigrants is making it real—and not just in border states. Latest census data show illegal immigrants increasing fast in Iowa, North Carolina, and Georgia.

I said this was big trouble for a couple of reasons. Economics was the first. The second is deeper. The situation we've created mocks American laws and ideals. It tells working, taxpaying citizens and other legal residents with Social Security numbers that they're chumps. Go to the emergency room, and if you can't pay your bill, the hospital can track you down and garnish your wages. But the illegal immigrant can't be tracked and doesn't pay the bill. You pay it, through your taxes. You dope.

The problem is so exquisitely complicated you get dizzy. The border is too big to barricade, and besides, isn't it a good thing when

Estimated Federal Taxes and Costs by Household, 2002

Illegal immigrants pay less in taxes, but still use government services and programs, thus creating a deficit.

	Average Federal Tax Payment	Average Federal Fiscal Costs	Fiscal Balance
All Non-Illegal Households	$15,099	$15,101	$(2)
Illegal Alien Households	$4,212	$6,949	$(2,737)

Source: Center for Immigration Studies analysis of March 2003 Current Population Survey.

people come to America wanting to work hard? Of course, unless they're after your job. But hasn't virtually every business and consumer benefited from all that cheap labor? And so on.

No wonder politicians refuse to go near this. But they'll have to. Hospitals in border states are closing. The taxpaying chumps are getting angry. The issue nobody wants to touch is about to make itself felt.

EVALUATING THE AUTHOR'S ARGUMENT:

Colvin says the politicians must begin to solve the problem of illegal immigration. However, in the previous viewpoint Pickel and Kempner note that past legislation was ineffective, and he suggests that future legislation would only slow down illegal immigration temporarily. If illegal immigration cannot be stopped, as Geller suggests, how can new laws solve this problem, as Colvin proposes? What kinds of laws would you suggest to solve this problem?

Viewpoint

5

The Economic Benefits of Illegal Immigration Outweigh Costs

"Are Americans willing to pay $4 instead of $1 for a head of lettuce?"

Greg James

Greg James is the CEO of Topic Entertainment, a Washington-based software company. In this opinion piece James argues that illegal immigrants benefit the U.S. economy and that a more pragmatic approach to the immigration controversy would acknowledge the fact that undocumented workers benefit the economy by keeping prices low.

AS YOU READ, CONSIDER THE FOLLOWING QUESTIONS:

1. Why are so many members of his own party criticizing the president's immigration policy?

2. According to James, what California industry most benefits from illegal immigration?

3. What kinds of immigrants does the author say are encouraged to cross the border illegally?

Greg James, "A Pragmatic Approach to Illegal Immigration," *The Seattle Times*, June 17, 2005. Copyright © 2005 The Seattle Times Company. Reproduced by permission of the author.

Sometimes you hear a discussion or debate in which the participants seem to be getting nowhere, don't understand the subject and can't see the obvious. A prime example of this is the illegal-immigration controversy, and the folks making lots of noise are on conservative talk radio.

The conversations on the subject usually revolve around two main themes: The president has sold out his conservative base, and he is ignoring national security by allowing illegal aliens to swarm over the border. . . . About the only thing they're ever right about on this contentious subject is that if the U.S. government wanted to do something about illegal immigration, it could. The truth, of course, is that the government doesn't want to do anything about it—and for good reason.

Illegal Immigrants Keep Business Costs Down

Our somewhat lax and paradoxical border policy is driven by something very basic: money and economics. A decade ago, there was a big fuss in California when some concerned citizens decided that the illegal immigrants in their state were a big strain on the budget, and were draining billions of dollars from education and health care.

The logic went that if the illegal aliens were stopped from sending their kids to school, and using free medicine, the state would save lots of money that it could then spend on its legal citizens.

An interesting thing happened next. Someone else did a follow-up study, and found that what the state saved in economic costs from the use of migrant labor in agriculture was over three times what it cost in health care and education to those same workers. In other words, illegal aliens were not costing the state a thing, but were instead saving the state tens of billions of dollars a year—and, at the same time, were keeping California's agricultural industry competitive with the rest of the world. The big fuss quietly went away and nothing much changed in California.

The right way to look at illegal immigration is with a pragmatic eye. Simple questions need to be asked: Are Americans willing to

> **FAST FACT**
>
> According to a June 2006 Gallup poll, 67 percent of U.S. adults think that immigration benefits the United States.

Protestors on both sides of the issue can be seen demonstrating for or against leniency with those who have come to the country illegally.

pay $4 instead of $1 for a head of lettuce? Do we really want to shore up the borders and then watch inflation grow rapidly? The big owners of agribusiness know the answer to these questions, as do the politicians they support. So we're stuck with this silly issue that won't go away, and with people who talk tough, but really wouldn't want the situation to change if they realized what the true costs to our economy and society would be.

Just the Right Number of Illegal Immigrants

I think I'd even go one step further and speculate that not only do people in high places understand this issue very well, they've probably got it worked out so that the illegal immigration that is happening is happening in just the right amounts. Consider how our Southern border is currently monitored: The Border Patrol stays close to the big cities and population centers, then thins out in rural areas and the desert. A coincidence? Doubtful. This policy effectively weeds out the weak and makes the trip tough enough that it discourages families and small children (bad for the U.S. economy), and makes the difficult passage overland a journey that mostly young males would be willing to risk (good for the U.S. economy).

In essence, you have a system that encourages the most desirable illegal immigrants, and discourages the rest. Americans then get the best of both worlds: cheap labor to do the backbreaking work that most in this society wouldn't want to do, and a competitive price for fresh fruits, vegetables and many other things dependent on manual labor.

As a bonus, if the "illegals" cause trouble, they can be deported without enjoying any of the rights a U.S. citizen would enjoy. It's really a pretty simple (if somewhat cynical) deal. And this president knows it, as do all the big ranchers, fruit farmers, grocers and restaurant owners who support him.

What's more, it would appear obvious, looking at recent history, that several presidents before George W. Bush figured out the same thing. To care about national security is to often make compromises. In this case, the angry voice of conservatives in his own party is the price this president pays for continuing a policy that, while difficult to actually articulate, really makes quite good sense.

EVALUATING THE AUTHOR'S ARGUMENT:

James does not include any statistics to back up his argument that illegal immigrants actually save states money by filling jobs at lower wages. How important are the lack of statistics in deciding the validity of his argument? What other information do you think might make James's argument stronger? James also points out that the placement of border guards is designed to allow only the strongest people to enter illegally. Does his evidence support this assertion? Explain.

The Economic Costs of Illegal Immigration Outweigh Benefits

"There is a pretty clear consensus that the fiscal impact of immigration depends on the education level of the immigrants."

Steven A. Camarota

Steven A. Camarota is the director of research at the Center for Immigration Studies. In his congressional testimony, Camarota explains that immigants with more education earn more money and pay more taxes to the government. However, most illegal immigrants have less education and pay less tax, but their children, who are often U.S. citizens, consume more government services, thus creating a deficit.

AS YOU READ, CONSIDER THE FOLLOWING QUESTIONS:

1. Which households does Camarota say had the higher percentage of adults who were employed: illegal immigrants, legal immigrants, or native-born citizens?

2. According to Camarota, which government program has higher than average use by illegal immigrants?

3. Which two government programs show a positive effect because of illegal immigration, according to the author?

Steven A. Camarota, "Immigration's Impact on Public Coffers," testimony prepared for the House Ways and Means Committee, July 26, 2006. www.cis.org/articles/2006/sactestimony072606.html.

Illegal Immigration Facts

- The Center for Immigration Studies (CIS) estimates that in 2002 illegal alien households imposed costs of $26 billion on the federal government and paid $16 billion in federal taxes, creating an annual net fiscal deficit of $10.4 billion at the federal level, or $2,700 per household.

- Among the largest costs were Medicaid ($2.5 billion); treatment for the uninsured ($2.2 billion); food assistance programs such as food stamps, WIC, and free school lunches ($1.9 billion); the federal prison/court systems ($1.6 billion); and federal aid to schools ($1.4 billion).

- If illegal aliens were legalized and began to pay taxes and use services like households headed by legal immigrants with the same education levels, CIS estimates the annual net fiscal deficit would increase to $29 billion, or $7,700 per household.

- The primary reason illegal aliens create a fiscal deficit is that an estimated 60 percent lack a high school degree and another 20 percent have no education beyond high school. The fiscal drain is not due to their legal status or unwillingness to work.

- Illegal aliens with little education are a significant fiscal drain, but less-educated immigrants who are legal residents are a much larger fiscal problem because they are eligible for many more programs.

- Many of the costs associated with illegal aliens are due to their US-born children who have American citizenship. Thus, barring illegal aliens themselves from federal programs will have little impact on costs.

- Focusing just on Social Security and Medicare, CIS estimates that illegal households create a combined net benefit for these two programs in excess of $7 billion a year. However, they create a net deficit of $17 billion in the rest of the budget, for a total net federal cost of $10 billion.

The Cost of Illegal Immigration

Immigration's impact on public coffers has long been at the center of the immigration debate. Until recently, however, we actually had

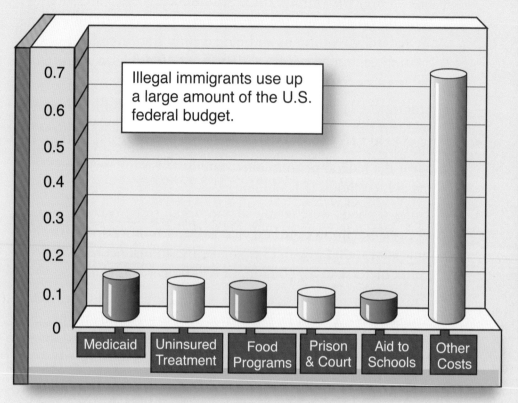

Distribution of $26.3 Billion in Costs of Illegal Immigration

Illegal immigrants use up a large amount of the U.S. federal budget.

Medicaid	Uninsured Treatment	Food Programs	Prison & Court	Aid to Schools	Other Costs

Source: Steven A. Camarota, Center for Immigration Studies.

very little reliable data on the subject. While there is still much that is not known, we now have some reasonably good information about this important topic. . . . There is a pretty clear consensus that the fiscal impact of immigration depends on the education level of the immigrants. Certainly other factors also matter, but the human capital of immigrants, as economists like to refer to it, is clearly very important. There is no single better predictor of one's income, tax payments or use of public services in modern America than one's education level. The vast majority of immigrants come as adults, and it should come as no surprise that the education they bring with them is a key determinant of their fiscal impact. It is simply not possible to fund social programs, including those for retirees, by bringing in large numbers of immigrants with relatively little education and resulting low incomes. . . .

Illegal Immigrants and the Federal Budget

A good deal of research has focused on the effect illegal [immigrants] have on taxpayers at the state and local level. Much of this work has examined only costs, or only tax payments, but not both. In my work I have tried to estimate both, and I have focused on the federal government. . . . Based on a detailed analysis of Census Bureau data, my analysis indicates that households headed by illegal aliens imposed more than $26.3 billion in costs on the federal government in 2002 and paid $16 billion in taxes, creating a net fiscal deficit of almost $10.4 billion, or $2,700 per illegal household. The largest costs are Medicaid ($2.5 billion); treatment for the uninsured ($2.2 billion); food assistance programs such as food stamps, WIC, and free school lunches ($1.9 billion); the federal prison and court systems ($1.6 billion); and federal aid to schools ($1.4 billion). . . .

> **FAST FACT**
>
> The Centers for Medicare and Medicaid Services estimate that the federal government spends $250 million every year reimbursing states for emergency medical care to illegal immigrants.

While the net fiscal drain they create for the federal government is significant, I also found that the costs illegal households impose on federal coffers are less than half that of other households, but their tax payments are only one-fourth that of other households. Many of the costs associated with illegals are due to their American-born children, who are awarded U.S. citizenship at birth. Thus, greater efforts to bar illegals from federal programs will not reduce costs because their citizen children can continue to access them. It must also be remembered that the vast majority of illegals hold jobs. Thus the fiscal deficit they create for the federal government is not the result of an unwillingness to work. In 2002, I found that 89 percent of illegal households had at least one person working compared to 78 percent of households headed by legal immigrants and natives. . . .

Many of the preconceived notions about the fiscal impact of illegal households turn out to be inaccurate. In terms of welfare use, receipt of cash assistance programs tends to be very low, while Medicaid use, though significant, is still less than for other households. Only use of food assistance programs is significantly higher than that of the rest of the population. Also, contrary to the perceptions that illegal aliens don't pay payroll taxes, we estimate that more than half of illegals work "on the books." On average, illegal households pay more than $4,200 a year in all forms of federal taxes. Unfortunately, they impose costs of $6,950 per household. . . .

As for Social Security and Medicare, our findings show that illegals have an unambiguously positive effect for these two programs. We estimate that illegal households create a combined net benefit for these two programs in excess of $7 billion a year, accounting for about 4 percent of the total annual surplus in these two programs. Unfortunately, they create a net drain of $17 billion in the rest of

Investigating the legal status of immigrants requires resources beyond what the immigration service can provide and the additional expense often falls to county governments.

the federal budget, for a total net loss of more than $10 billion. Nonetheless, their impact on Social Security and Medicare is unquestionably positive. . . .

We Cannot Afford Less-Educated Immigrants

If you take nothing else away from my testimony, it should be remembered that it simply is not possible to fund social programs, including those for retirees, by bringing in large numbers of immigrants with relatively little education. This is central to the debate over illegal immigration . . . because 60 percent of illegals are estimated to have not completed high school and another 20 have only a high school degree. The fiscal problem created by less-educated immigrants exists even though the vast majority of immigrants, including illegals, work and did not come to America to get welfare. The realities of the modern American economy coupled with the modern American administrative state make large fiscal costs an unavoidable problem of large scale less-educated immigration.

This fact does not reflect a moral defect on the part of immigrants. What it does mean is that we need an immigration policy that reflects the reality of modern America. We may decide to let illegals stay and we may even significantly increase the number of less-educated legal immigrants allowed into the country. . . . But we have to at least understand that such a policy will create large unavoidable costs for taxpayers.

EVALUATING THE AUTHOR'S ARGUMENT:

Camarota's research contradicts Greg James's assertion in the previous article that illegal immigrants actually save states money by filling lower-paying jobs. Based on the evidence presented in these two articles, which argument do you think is the better one? What evidence supports the better argument?

Chapter 2

Who Should Enforce U.S. Immigration Laws?

Public health workers are one of the groups states are targeting to help identify and deny services to illegal immigrants.

Local Police Should Enforce Immigration Laws

"'Alabama welcomes those who enter the country legally, but we won't stand idly by and do nothing when we catch illegal immigrants in our state.'"

Miriam Jordan

Miriam Jordan is a reporter for the *Wall Street Journal.* In this article Jordan reports on a growing trend in which city and state police officers are receiving extra training that will allow them to assist the Immigration and Customs Enforcement unit of Homeland Security in enforcing immigration laws.

AS YOU READ, CONSIDER THE FOLLOWING QUESTIONS:

1. How many weeks of training are local police required to take before they are trained in immigrant law enforcement?

2. The program to train local police officers to enforce immigration laws was created in 1996, but no state signed on to participate for several years. What event led the first state to join this federal program, according to Jordan?

3. According to the legislative counsel for the International Association of Chiefs of Police, what kinds of problems might result when local police enforce immigration laws?

Miriam Jordan, "The New Immigration Cops: Cities and States Take on Difficult Duty of Handling Undocumented Workers," *The Wall Street Journal,* February 2, 2006, p. B1. Copyright © 2006, Dow Jones & Company Inc. Republished with permission of *The Wall Street Journal.*

In Alabama, about 160 illegal immigrants have been arrested since the state entered a special partnership in 2003 with the Immigration and Customs Enforcement unit of Homeland Security, or ICE as it is known. Under this arrangement, police officers . . . are specially trained in some immigration enforcement duties. Alabama decided to join the program because local officials believed ICE's small staff in the state was unable to cope with the swelling numbers of illegal immigrants. Last fall, Gov. Bob Riley pledged to double the number of state troopers trained to deal with illegal immigrants, saying: "Alabama welcomes those who enter the country legally, but we won't stand idly by and do nothing when we catch illegal immigrants in our state."

Program Details

Forty-four of the 650 state troopers in the state, a figure that includes administrative and field officers, have taken the five-week training course and are now authorized to enforce federal immigration law. That training involves detecting false identification, understanding the details of federal immigration law as well as the pitfalls of racial profiling and other possible civil-rights violations. The ICE partnership empowers local officers to temporarily detain someone who has violated federal immigration law—something that they are typically not allowed to do. That is a valuable tool in states where there are few ICE agents. The trained officers usually don't participate in sweeps or actively search for illegal immigrants; the emphasis is on human smugglers and convicted felons that officers come across during the course of their duties.

The federal program to train local police officers in such duties has existed since 1996. Florida, the first state to join the federal program in the wake of the Sept. 11, 2001 terrorist attacks, tailored its version to help block possible terrorist infiltrators. Interest in the program has taken off recently as the national debate over illegal immigration has heated up. In recent months, ICE has received requests from

> **FAST FACT**
>
> According to an April 2006 edition of the *Los Angeles Times*, returning to Mexico is so dangerous that only 20 percent of illegal immigrants try to return to their native country.

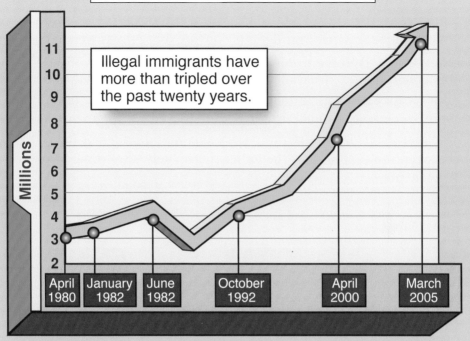

Total Unauthorized Migrants Living in the United States

Illegal immigrants have more than tripled over the past twenty years.

Millions

11
10
9
8
7
6
5
4
3
2

| April 1980 | January 1982 | June 1982 | October 1992 | April 2000 | March 2005 |

Source: Pew Hispanic Center (2005).

several states in New England and the Midwest, as well as counties in Texas and California, which are interested in immigration training. "It has proven very difficult for the federal government to increase manpower in the enforcement of immigration law fast enough," says Kris Kobach, a law professor at the University of Missouri, Kansas City, who oversaw the application of the program when he served as counsel to the U.S. attorney general from 2001 to 2003. "This provision allows those states that want to help to fill in the gap."

Not All Communities Agree with Program

The ICE program has sparked emotional debate in some regions. In December, the city council of Costa Mesa in southern California became the latest jurisdiction to decide to enter the ICE program. Mayor Allan Mansoor, who proposed joining, said the initiative would designate specialized officers, such as gang specialists and investigators, to do immigration checks. The program's primary focus would be on identifying criminals. Mr. Mansoor, who is also a deputy sheriff of Orange County, estimates that 10% to 15% of all inmates in the county's jails are illegal immigrants. He said that many undocumented immigrants convicted of crimes were released into the streets of the U.S. after serving their prison term rather than being sent home. "We want to make sure they are deported," he said. But Costa Mesa wasn't unanimously behind the mayor. Before the vote, several city council meetings were rocked by opponents shouting that the plan was discriminatory and would undercut fragile ties between immigrants and the police. Ultimately, the council voted 3 to 2 in favor.

In some places the National Guard and local police have been brought in to help patrol the country's borders.

Some police organizations and human-rights groups are concerned that deputizing local officers to handle immigration enforcement might violate civil liberties—and undermine safety. "A key concern is that state and local enforcement involvement in immigration can have a chilling effect on the relationship with the immigrant community in their jurisdiction," says Gene Voegtlin, legislative counsel for the International Association of Chiefs of Police. That could lead immigrants to become reluctant to report crimes or cooperate with officers investigating incidents. . . .

Some [critics] worry that the federal government is trying to spread the burden of rounding up illegal immigrants at a time when state and local police departments are already strapped for resources. Virginia Kice, an ICE spokeswoman, stresses that the program is entirely voluntary. "We are not going out and soliciting participation," she says. But, "we are receiving inquiries from all over the country."

Los Angeles Mayor Antonio Villaraigosa recently said that the city wouldn't follow the lead of Costa Mesa and involve police officers in identifying illegal immigrants. However, civilian jail personnel in Los Angeles and San Bernardino counties who have undergone ICE training are screening foreign-born inmates to determine whether they can be deported, according to an ICE spokeswoman.

EVALUATING THE AUTHOR'S ARGUMENT:

In her report Jordan writes that federal immigration agencies have not been able to increase manpower fast enough to handle the increase in illegal immigration that has occurred in recent years. The expectation is that local police can help fill the void. Assuming this statement to be true, should local police be a permanent part of immigration enforcement? If not permanent, how long should local police assume these temporary immigration duties?

If Local Police Enforce the Borders It Will Lead to Racial Profiling

"Once street officers become surrogate immigration agents, all is lost."

Ruben Navarrette

Ruben Navarrette, a columnist and editorial board member of the *San Diego Union-Tribune*, is a nationally syndicated columnist with the Washington Post Writers Group. In this opinion piece Navarrette warns of the dangers that lie with using local police to enforce immigration laws. Instead, according to Navarrette, employers who hire illegal immigrants should be charged with breaking the law.

AS YOU READ, CONSIDER THE FOLLOWING QUESTIONS:

1. What is the title of the proposed law that would permit local police to begin enforcing U.S. immigration laws?
2. Which U.S. city became the first city to begin using local police as a tool for immigration law enforcement?
3. What does Navarrette propose as an alternative method of dealing with illegal immigration?

Ruben Navarrette, "Misguided Border Patrolling," *USA Today*, February 15, 2006, p. 13A. Reproduced by permission of the author.

Because I'm not just the grandson of a Mexican immigrant but also the son of a retired cop, my views on illegal immigration are complicated. I'm convinced that immigrants—whatever their status—are America's most valuable import. Yet I wasn't raised to take lightly things such as border security or the breaking of laws.

The trouble is that some proposed solutions—from putting troops on the border to denying citizenship to the children of illegal immigrants—bring to mind the old saying about the cure being worse than the disease. That includes this one: Allowing local police to enforce federal immigration law.

This dangerous and self-defeating concept is popular with those who think that law enforcement officers are interchangeable, and that one badge is as good as another. As proponents of this approach see it, police chase down criminals (including illegal immigrants) and it makes no difference whether their jurisdiction is local, state or federal. Some advocates even want to require local police to enforce immigration law—something opposed by many police associations, including the International Association of Chiefs of Police. The Clear Law Enforcement for Criminal Alien Removal (CLEAR) Act, introduced in 2003 by Rep. Charles Norwood, R[Republican]-Ga., and reintroduced in 2005, would enlist state and local law enforcement agencies in the enforcement of federal immigration laws.

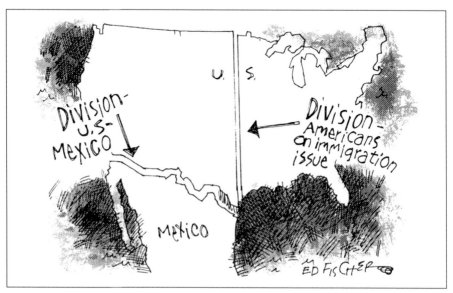

Who Should Enforce U.S. Immigration Laws? 57

This Is the Wrong Answer

A mandate from Washington would be the worst possible thing. This is a decision best left to local and state authorities. We can only hope they make the right one.

In Costa Mesa, Calif., city officials recently made the wrong decision. At the urging of Mayor Allan Mansoor, the City Council in December [2005] voted to authorize local police officers to be trained to enforce immigration law. That makes Costa Mesa, which is an hour's drive south of Los Angeles, the first city in the USA to take this road.

It probably won't be the last. State police agencies in Florida and Alabama and the county sheriff's department in Orange County, where Costa Mesa is located, have sought a "memorandum of un-

Some fear that, because approaches and training can vary greatly, racial profiling could become a problem if local police forces are expected to enforce immigration laws.

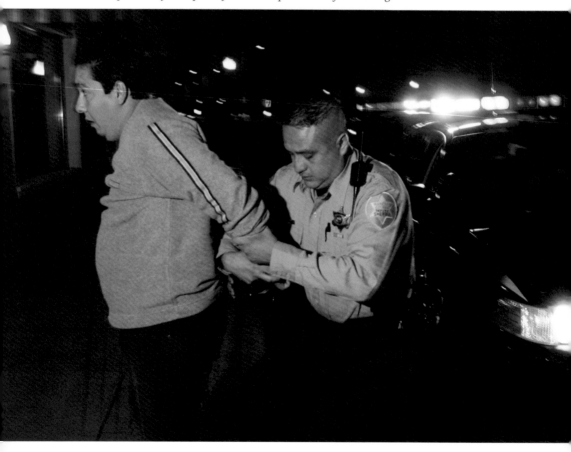

derstanding" from the U.S. Immigration and Customs Enforcement agency to train their officers to enforce immigration law. An official at ICE told *USA Today* that there are at least 10 more pending inquiries from local authorities in New England, the South and the Midwest—all of them aiming to take immigration law into their own hands.

In Costa Mesa, officials seem to want a crackdown limited to what Mansoor calls "criminal offenders," or suspects of wrongdoing beyond entering the country illegally. That includes gang activity. In fact, it's significant that of the first 40 officers for whom the city wants to seek training, most are detectives, gang specialists and jail personnel. Mansoor says that there won't be any sweeps or raids on employers, and that police will not be targeting illegal immigrants.

Those are some silver linings. Another would be if Costa Mesa's experiment excluded beat cops. Once street officers become surrogate immigration agents, all is lost. Whatever amount of trust the police department has built with immigrant communities will deteriorate. The possibility of racial profiling will increase. An initiative intended to combat crime could easily backfire and fuel it instead if immigrants are too scared to report crimes committed against them. . . .

The Root of the Problem

Let's not forget how Costa Mesa found itself in this predicament. Mansoor says that it's because the federal government has failed to do its duty.

Nonsense. If illegal immigrants are congregating in Costa Mesa—and thousands of U.S. cities like it—there's only one reason. It's because people in those places have decided they cannot live without the cheap and readily available labor supplied by illegal immigrants. Those are the real culprits—the teachers and engineers and soccer moms who love that they can afford upper-class perks (nannies, gardeners and housekeepers) on middle-class wages. Those are the folks

Mansoor and the city should crack down on if they want to solve this problem. At least one other city in California has tried issuing fines to employers who pluck day laborers off streets.

Personally, the cop's son in me would like to see a three-strikes law: The first time you hire an illegal immigrant, you get a warning. The second time, you get a $10,000 fine. The third, you get a week in jail. Currently, the law says you're not in trouble unless you "knowingly" hire an illegal immigrant. But after your third offense, shouldn't you be in the know? Americans want to get tough on illegal immigrants. Fine. But you can't do that without first getting tough on those who hire them.

I'm probably naive. Politicians know what they can get away with and what they can't. Immigrants who don't vote and can't speak English are not a threat. But employers of cheap labor who are singled out for prosecution can retaliate by spending money to defeat politicians and elect their opponents. That part isn't complicated. Never has been.

EVALUATING THE AUTHOR'S ARGUMENT:

In the previous viewpoint Miriam Jordan endorses the use of local police as a way to alleviate a shortage of immigration agents. But in this viewpoint Ruben Navarrette argues that there are better ways to deal with illegal immigration than using local police agencies. Which writer presents the stronger argument? What evidence do you find most compelling? What problems do you see with the argument that you judge is the weaker of the two arguments presented?

"Why shouldn't police—or teachers, or emergency workers, for that matter —lend overwhelmed immigration officials a hand?"

Employees Who Work in Service Industries Should Determine Residency Status

Douglas McGray

Douglas McGray is a California-based writer and a fellow at the New America Foundation. In this article McGray presents information about the efforts that many individual states are making to ease the illegal immigration problem, including requiring that ordinary police, teachers, and medical personnel must report any contact with illegal immigrants. In some cases failure to report illegal immigrants would be a crime.

Douglas McGray, "Shift Work: Should Policing Illegal Immigrants Fall to Nurses and Teachers?" *The Washington Monthly*, vol. 38, April 2006, p. 17–21. Copyright © 2006 by Washington Monthly Publishing, LLC, 733 15th St. NW, Suite 520, Washington DC 20005. (202) 393-5155. Website: www.washington monthly.com. Reproduced by permission.

AS YOU READ, CONSIDER THE FOLLOWING QUESTIONS:

1. What reason is given by many citizens for the increased need of public workers to help enforce immigration laws?
2. What do Massachusetts, Georgia, Kentucky, New York, and Virginia have in common, as they struggle with the issue of providing services to the children of illegal immigrants?
3. How did California's Proposition 187 combat illegal immigrants?

Just an hour from San Francisco, on the road to Fresno, a rancher has sheared a giant cross, and the words "Jesus Saves," into a grassy hillside. A little farther south, a National Rifle Association banner billows from a long truck bed, parked by the side of Route 99 until harvest time. Away from California's big cities and the cool Pacific coast lies a flat, fertile landscape that's politically more like Indiana than Marin County. Here, in California's Central Valley, U.S. citizens and illegal, undocumented immigrants have lived in a kind of awkward partnership for decades. As they do business now, the region's lucrative commercial farms (the foundation of an otherwise shaky economy) would shut down without undocumented labor. Yet the cultural impact of that huge undocumented workforce remains a sore point with conservative locals. . . .

The Role of Public Workers

Undocumented workers cannot, by law have drivers' licenses, and virtually none has insurance. So Fresno's cops spend a great deal of time busting illegal immigrants for traffic violations and impounding their cars. Every farm worker you talk to seems to have had a car impounded for driving without a license, many, more than once, and each incident brings fines and fees that can equal a month's salary—a huge blow. "They're running the gauntlet each time they're out on the road," [police captain Pat] Farmer says, not unsympathetically. But while many illegal workers feel targeted by traffic cops, it is significant what the police refuse to do: turn them in to federal immigration authorities.

"We don't enforce immigration laws," Farmer tells me firmly. "We care about behavior. It's not where you're from, it's what you're doing," And that is official: local ordinances bar Fresno cops from so much as making small talk about immigration status, a policy police veterans like Farmer strongly support. . . .

Procedures that make sense to cops on the beat may seem ridiculous to many citizens. Why shouldn't police—or teachers, or emergency workers, for that matter—lend overwhelmed immigration officials a hand? Federal agents arrested more than a million people trying to cross in 2004; still, the number of illegal immigrants living in the United States has grown by 23 percent during the first half of this decade, according to a recent Pew Hispanic Center study, and some half a million more take up residence each year. . . .

How to Solve the Problem

Until recently, most Americans lived in communities where few (if any) illegal immigrants settled. Conditions were ideal for a policy of willful inattention. But that's changing, as immigrants—legal and illegal—increasingly settle throughout the country. California's share of the country's estimated 10 million illegal residents is shrinking, as dozens of states from Virginia to Idaho see their undocumented populations explode. In a handful of these new immigration hubs, more than half of the foreign-born population is now undocumented. . . .

Congress and the president have finally begun to talk about overhauling the slow, dysfunctional legal immigration system, which drives honest job seekers underground, and putting enforcement at the border that does more than just divert people into a lethal desert. But they have found no meaningful consensus on how to do it. The Republican House may agree to throw more money at the Department of Homeland Security or slap illegal immigrants with heavier penalties, but this is the legislative version of looking busy. Both President Bush and Sen. Edward Kennedy (D[Democrat]-Mass.) have campaigned for an approach that mixes new options for immigrant laborers with beefed-up enforcement, but neither has made much headway.

As a result, state and community leaders are rushing into the void. Since last year, legislators in 21 states, from New York to Alabama, have debated dozens of bills designed to deputize public employees for a new kind of immigration fight. To them, it seems obvious that local cops should detain illegal immigrants for deportation. It seems pragmatic to encourage local emergency rooms to patch up anyone who is

Attitudes Toward Immigration

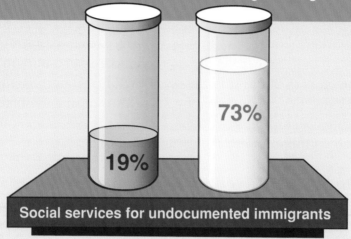

In this survey, 73% of those polled want the government to spend less on social services for illegal immigrants.

73%

19%

Social services for undocumented immigrants

Source: Social Research Laboratory, Northern Arizona University.

seriously ill or injured, but insist that they turn other undocumented immigrants away, and maybe even share patient data with immigration officials. Just about anyone who collects a city, county, or state paycheck could do a little immigration work on the side. . . .

Legislators in Colorado and Alabama have proposed a mandatory citizenship check for all public services, except in cases of emergency. Federal law already requires proof of citizenship for the really expensive stuff, like Medicaid and welfare, or states have no choice but to make it universally available (public education through high school, urgent medical treatment, incarceration), so these proposals mostly build enforcement into less obvious programs: vaccinations for the poor, after-school tutoring, prenatal care, even hunting and fishing licenses. Florida and South Carolina have debated a bill to require undocumented immigrants to pay for any non-emergency hospital care in advance. Idaho lawmakers have proposed banning them from all county health services, unless the county agrees to deport patients once they are well, and pay the deportation bill. . . .

Almost any public institution could be deputized. Some officials in Lowell, Mass., a diverse Boston suburb, want federal Department of Education permission to screen for illegal immigrants at the town's public vocational high school. Georgia, Kentucky, and New York have suggested barring undocumented immigrants from all state colleges, no matter how young they were when their parents brought them to the United States, and Virginia signed the idea into law. . . .

Everyone Would Report Illegal Immigrants

Then there are lawmakers who go even further—not only proposing to deny government services to illegal immigrants, but requiring that civil servants snitch on any they encounter, reporting them to federal immigration authorities. State legislators in Georgia, Alabama, North Carolina, Tennessee, and Maine have aimed to turn everyone from nurses and community-college professors to child-welfare workers and park rangers into the eyes and ears of federal immigration authorities. Arkansas and Tennessee lawmakers actually recommended charging local, county, and state employees with misdemeanors if they identify an illegal immigrant and fail to pass any intelligence they have to the feds—identical to the federal sentence for sneaking across the border. "Illegal immigrants have been given a safe haven in this state," the so-called Arkansas Taxpayer and Citizen Protection Act bristles.

All of these measures carry the genes of California's landmark Proposition 187, a 1994 ballot initiative that would have denied the state's undocumented immigrants access to any institution with taxpayer funding. It required doctors and elementary school teachers to turn in any illegal immigrants they identified, not just to turn them away. And it passed, with 59 percent of voters behind it. The measure fell apart after the federal courts ruled portions of it unconstitutional. But as undocumented immigrants have spread out from California since the early 1990s, so have the ideas embodied by Prop. 187. In the last election, Arizona voters passed a near copy of California's initiative, tailored to avoid the original's run-in with the courts. A delegation of Colorado state legislators

> **FAST FACT**
>
> The Journal of American Physicians and Surgeons reported in its spring 2005 issue that eighty-four California hospitals were closing their doors as a direct result of the rising number of illegal immigrants.

visited the initiative's authors in Arizona last fall, and promised to bring a version before Colorado voters in November. . . .

Not Everyone Agrees on More Enforcement

Many local lawmakers insist these measures will help. But overwhelmingly, if quietly, the nurses, professors, administrators, cops, and outreach workers that lawmakers seek to deputize resist the call. One by one, New York, Los Angeles, and an array of other cities have written policies like Fresno's, strictly forbidding police officers to inquire about immigration status. And last fall, when federal legislators demanded that hospitals collect two pages of immigration data from patients to access a $1-billion fund for uninsured care, doctors and hospital administrators, including the American Hospital Association and American Medical Association, revolted. These objections are mostly practical. Local immigration enforcement, they say, will damage communities, destroy lives, cost far more than supporters understand, and do little to stop illegal immigration.

The San Joaquin Health Center, 30 miles southwest of downtown Fresno, sits across the street from a seed warehouse, and a lot filled with aging farm machinery. There is a clinic just like it in many of the tiny, no-stoplight towns that appear without warning and disappear just as quickly in the vast, green orchards of the Central Valley. Every seat in the waiting room is full on the morning I visit. But it is usually this way. The clinic, small enough to pass for a house, has about 35,000 active patients.

Roughly half of those patients have at least a little health insurance, one doctor tells me, as he scribbles on a farm worker's chart. The rest have nothing, usually because they are undocumented. The clinic charges uninsured patients for services, on a sliding scale, but many never pay, and that is o.k., says the doctor. The organization manages to stay solvent with county, state, and federal grants.

Medical Personnel Know Who Is Illegally in the United States

This is just the sort of care that many state lawmakers seek to outlaw. And they are right about one thing: These doctors know hundreds, maybe thousands of undocumented immigrants in the community. "They'll be very open," says Rodrigo Dezubiria, a clinic doctor. "I snuck across the border, I snuck across five times." (At the county hospital in Fresno, administrators are even more systematic; they have the immigration status of tens of thousands of area residents stored in a confidential patient database.) But turning those patients away, or reporting them to the feds? "It's a simple-minded thing to suggest," says Dezubiria.

A week before my visit, an undocumented farm worker came to the clinic for the first time with gangrene creeping all the way up to his knee. It was a straightforward case of diabetes. Preventative care—the kind of treatment many state proposals would reserve for citizens—would have been easy and cheap. Instead, Dezubiria had to rush

Some states hope to involve all public workers in efforts to identify and deport illegal immigrants.

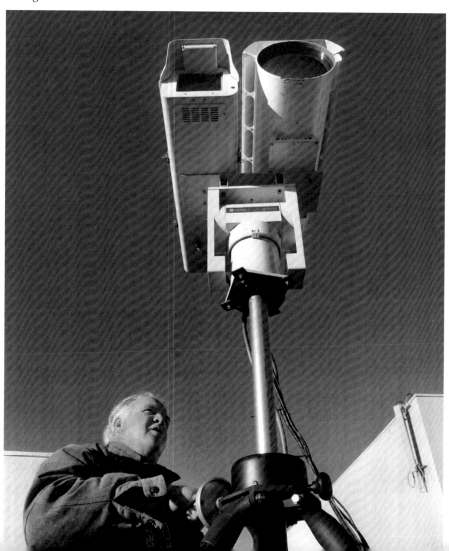

him to the hospital where surgeons amputated his leg, and absorbed an astronomical bill. "Pay now or pay later," Dezubiria shrugs. The expensive choice left a man disabled for life.

Community workers across professions share strikingly similar views of the dysfunction that would spread if state laws pulled them, or their colleagues, into immigration work. Sarah Reyes, director of Fresno's nonprofit food bank, explains that, as it is, welfare offices have a perennial problem getting enough undocumented immigrants to show up. We walk past row after row of Fig Newtons and Ritz Crackers, Caesar dressing and bananas. They don't qualify for food stamps, she explains, but their American-born kids do. First, though, everyone in the household faces a detailed interview and digital fingerprint scan. If word got out that the welfare office reported immigration violations, they would never reach those American kids—more than a million under age 6, nationally, according to a recent study by the nonprofit Urban Institute. . . .

Many People Support More Enforcement by Public Workers

To many citizens, it makes no sense that thousands of illegal immigrants routinely come to the attention of public officials without consequences. Local lawmakers have tapped into that frustration, even encouraged it. Not only do these laws make it harder for civil servants to do their jobs, but even federal immigration officials are, at best, ambivalent about this kind of help.

As chief of the local Immigration and Customs Enforcement office, Brian Poulson is the Department of Homeland Security's senior immigration enforcer in central California, a post he has held since the 1990s, when his office was called the INS. Lawmakers may be dreaming up new ways to tip Poulson and his team off to undocumented immigrants among them, but Poulson says his office is barely equipped to keep up with criminals and absconders and monitor potential terrorist targets like pipelines and airports.

"There are 45,000 people locked up in my area," he says. He estimates about 13,000 of them are eligible for deportation—and the jails often release them anyway, without warning his agents, when they run out of beds. "We are overwhelmed by that alone." Besides, he says, "we already get a tremendous amount of information from callers." Snooping neighbors, jilted boyfriends and girlfriends, people looking for the last word in an argument: They call all day long. "We have to tell them to write it down and send it in," Poulson says, "or we'd be on the phone all day." . . . "I think we've reached oversaturation," he says. "You could triple our staff, I'm not sure how much difference it would make." . . .

Congress [should take] the initiative back from states and locals. Of course, Congress will have to . . . work out some deep differences before states get any further ahead of them. And that may mean risking the ire of voters in an election year. The Americans most passionate about immigration politics are unlikely to accept a practical compromise, and they will mobilize against any official who offends them—by, say, offering a chance at citizenship to undocumented workers who settled here long ago, or putting muscular enforcement at the border. But an awkward issue for the reelection campaign is nothing to fear, compared with the dysfunction of a nationwide, piecemeal immigration system. No community will lie beyond its reach. "We are all border towns now," Poulson says wryly. "Even Washington, DC."

EVALUATING THE AUTHOR'S ARGUMENT:

McGray presents information about how many different states are trying to deal with the increasing numbers of illegal immigrants. Within his article it becomes clear that not everyone supports some of the more extreme measures, even though McGray suggests that the movement of illegal immigrants away from border communities has created added economic and social pressures on communities, which has to be resolved. In the viewpoint that follows, the author outlines the opposition to plans to make medical personnel immigration deputies. Which of the groups mentioned would you support becoming involved in policing illegal immigration: local police, teachers, or medical personnel?

Employees Who Work in Service Industries Should Not Determine Residency Status

"'It is the concern of emergency health care providers that the Illegal Immigration Control Act would criminalize emergency nurses and physicians.'"

Legislative Network for Nurses

In this anonymous editorial, the author writes that the Emergency Nurses Association and the American College of Emergency Physicians are very opposed to any change in the law that would force doctors and nurses to report illegal immigrants or face criminal changes.

AS YOU READ, CONSIDER THE FOLLOWING QUESTIONS:

1. Why are emergency health care workers concerned about the language in Section 202 of HR 4437, according to the author?

"Emergency Nurses Oppose Language in Immigration Bill," *Legislative Network for Nurses*, vol. 23, April 10, 2006, p. 51. Copyright © 2006 Business Publishers, Inc. Reproduced by permission.

2. What is the current law regarding emergency treatment for immigrants?
3. What action is the Emergency Nurses Association (ENA) urging in their letter?

Emergency nurses and other providers would find it more difficult to do their jobs if the Illegal Immigration Control Act is passed, Nancy Bonalumi, president of the Emergency Nurses Association, told LNN. "It is the concern of emergency health care providers that the Illegal Immigration Control Act would criminalize emergency nurses and physicians," Bonalumi, said. Under the bill, any nurse or physician abiding by the Emergency Medical Treatment and Labor Act (EMTALA) might technically be harboring, aiding or "smuggling" illegal immigrants, she added.

Letter Sent to Senator

The ENA and American College of Emergency Physicians wrote a letter dated March 28, 2006, to Sen. Arlen Specter (R-Pa.), chairman of the Judiciary Committee, expressing their concern regarding Section 202 of the Border Protection, Antiterrorism, and Illegal Immigration Control Act of 2005 (H.R. 4437), as passed by the House.

The letter states, "We understand that a comparable provision to Section 202 has been included in the bill reported out by the Senate Judiciary Committee. We believe this language could inadvertently place our members and their hospitals in untenable positions while attempting to comply with existing federal laws."

Under current federal law—the Emergency Medical Treatment and Labor Act—hospitals participating in Medicare must medically screen all persons seeking emergency

> **FAST FACT**
>
> A 2002 study by MGT of America reports that many Southwest border hospitals are having trouble recruiting physicians for their emergency departments because of liability issues related to the Emergency Medical Treatment and Labor Act.

Police officers are among those who some are calling on to identify the residency of immigrants with questionable legal status.

care regardless of their citizenship or immigration status. Those individuals who are found to need emergency care must be provided treatment necessary to stabilize them, regardless of insurance coverage or ability to pay.

Additionally, Section 1011 of the 2003 Medicare Modernization Act reimburses hospitals and other providers for some of their uncompensated care costs for emergency services to undocumented immigrants. To obtain this reimbursement, providers must determine the residency status of the patients that they treat. Therefore, it is reasonable to expect that emergency department doctors and nurses are knowingly providing care to illegal immigrants, the ENA said.

Doctors and Nurses Could Be Criminals

Section 202 of H.R. 4437 expands current law in defining "smuggling" activities subject to prosecution under federal law, the letter says. The House bill similarly criminalizes anyone who attempts to provide assistance or harbors an illegal immigrant. "Our concern is that providing needed and legally required health care to an illegal alien could meet this definition and, thereby, criminalize the care provided by our nurses and doctors. Health care providers and hospitals could not function under such conflicting mandates," the letter added.

[The Emergency Nurses Association and the American College of Emergency Physicians write that they] "strongly urge the Senate to complete action on a bill which excludes Section 202 or any comparable language. We look forward to working with you to ensure that our emergency nurses and physicians can continue to fulfill their mission and comply with federal mandates to care for all who enter an emergency department."

EVALUATING THE AUTHOR'S ARGUMENT:

The previous article also suggests that public workers who do not reveal the status of an illegal immigrant might be subject to legal action. Based on this information, do you think that criminalizing the actions of nurses, doctors, or even teachers, would help solve the problem of illegal immigration?

Chapter 3

What Is the Best Way to Solve the Illegal Immigration Problem?

Many undocumented adults come to the United States looking for better circumstances in which to raise their children.

Amnesty and Guest Worker Programs Would Solve the Illegal Immigration Problem

"From 1990 to 2000, illegal immigration increased by 5.5 million."

Cesar Conda and Stuart Anderson

Cesar Conda has served as Vice President Dick Cheney's domestic policy adviser. Stuart Anderson is a former staff director of the Senate Immigration Subcommittee and is the executive director of the National Foundation for American Policy. In this article Conda and Anderson argue that President George W. Bush's plan to impose fines and offer temporary visas for immigrants who are in the United States illegally would eliminate illegal immigration, since it would offer immigrants a legal way to enter the country to find work.

AS YOU READ, CONSIDER THE FOLLOWING QUESTIONS:

1. Why is it so difficult for foreign nationals to get temporary visas to work in the United States, according to the authors?
2. How many immigrants without college degrees are permitted green cards every year?
3. How many young men and women do the authors say die each year while trying to cross the border into the United States illegally?

Under President George W. Bush's plan, immigrant workers would no longer need to evade Border Patrol agents or die trying. Moreover, recognizing reality, the president would allow those now working illegally in this country to pay a fine and obtain a temporary visa, good for three years but renewable. Crucially, the president recognizes that "our current limits on legal immigration are too low," and he pledged to work with Congress "to increase the annual number of green cards."

Some History About Temporary Visas

A little background helps explain why this last point is so important. Contrary to some perceptions, current law is in practice highly restrictive in offering opportunities for U.S. employers to hire immigrants to work legally in agriculture and other non-professional fields. While H-2A visas for agricultural workers are uncapped, the procedure for obtaining them is so cumbersome and litigation-prone that fewer than 30,000 such visas are issued annually, while several hundred thousand immigrants work in the fields illegally. Though individuals may work in non-agricultural jobs under the H-2B visa, restrictive interpretations of the statute have generally prevented employers from hiring individuals for jobs other than those that are seasonal or of very short duration. In addition, that category is capped at 66,000 annually. An even lower cap limits sponsorship for permanent residence (green cards) to 10,000 per year for immigrants coming here to work who possess less than an undergraduate degree.

The absence of avenues to work legally in the United States is a primary reason for the current levels of illegal immigration. This can be seen clearly by looking back at the bracero program, which allowed foreign agricultural workers easier access to U.S. jobs. As the bracero program expanded in the 1950s, INS apprehensions of illegal immigrants fell from the 1953 level of 885,587 to as low as 45,336 in 1959—a 95 percent reduction in the flow of illegal immigration into the United States. From 1964—when the bracero program ended—to 1976, INS apprehensions increased from 86,597 to 875,915 (and have remained at roughly that level or higher ever since).

Amnesty and Guest Worker Programs

Whether Republican or Democrat, most Americans favor guest worker programs.

% Favor	Total (%)	Republican (%)	Democrat (%)
Allowing illegal immigrants to register as guest workers	79	79	77
Allowing illegal immigrants U.S. citizenship if they learn English, have a job, and pay taxes	78	73	82
Granting temporary visas to immigrants not in the United States so they can do seasonal/temporary work and return to home countries	72	72	71

Source: *Time* magazine poll was conducted by telephone between March 29 and March 30, 2006, among a national random sample of 1,004 adults, aged 18 and older throughout America.

This is not to say that workers who entered the bracero program did not experience problems or even hardships. The point is that when legal entry to work was widely permitted, illegal entry to the United States was an order of magnitude lower. And immigration enforcement officials understood this. At a congressional hearing in

Some Americans believe that because the illegal immigrants are here and willing to work that we should create a system that allows us to benefit from their labor.

the 1950s, a top INS official was asked about stopping illegal immigration if Mexican agricultural workers could no longer come in legally. He replied, "We can't do the impossible, Mr. Congressman."

Consequences of Doing Nothing

Congress can certainly choose to maintain the status quo, which is an enforcement-only approach. However, the evidence is strong that current policies—or even more hardened versions of them—are ineffective. From 1990 to 2000, illegal immigration increased by 5.5 million as the number of U.S. Border Patrol agents rose from 3,600 to nearly 10,000.

Existing policies also contribute to two unintended consequences: (1) More than 300 young men and women die each year trying to cross dangerous terrain or wade rivers. (2) The difficulty of an illegal crossing causes more migrants to stay in the United States after making it, rather than work for a short time and return to Mexico. . . .

The President's Proposal

Meanwhile, Bush's critics . . . are wrong on key aspects of the president's proposal.

This is not an amnesty. The definition of an amnesty is an unconditional pardon. Bush's proposal requires the payment of a fine and does not guarantee a green card to anyone. In contrast, the 1986 amnesty signed by President Reagan allowed permanent residence for anyone present in the country within certain dates.

FAST FACT

A March 2005 study by the Pew Hispanic Center reports that undocumented workers make up only 5 percent of the U.S. workforce.

The proposal is not a repeat of the 1986 law. In 1986, Congress largely wiped the slate clean but failed to provide any new mechanisms for individuals to enter and work legally, thus ensuring another buildup of the illegal population.

This is not the end of the American worker. Any temporary worker program will contain labor protections. Moreover, Americans who may now feel they compete unfairly with someone here illegally (who is thus too scared to make problems for the boss) will no longer face that problem. . . .

By combining enforcement with new temporary worker visas, the president's plan carries with it a tremendous opportunity to reduce illegal entry into the United States, freeing Border Patrol agents to focus on more serious concerns like terrorism. It would make controlling the border far more manageable and make known to authorities anyone seeking legal status.

EVALUATING THE AUTHORS' ARGUMENT:

Conda and Anderson suggest that enforcement is not the answer to the problem of illegal immigration and that offering temporary visas to immigrants will curb the number of illegal immigrants entering the United States. In the next article Mark Krikorian argues that guest worker programs are cumbersome to manage and that these programs do nothing to eliminate the possibility of terrorists entering illegally. Which argument do you think is the stronger and what evidence is the most persuasive in helping you make your decision?

Viewpoint

2

Amnesty and Guest Worker Programs Would Not Solve the Illegal Immigration Problem

"The result of placing the huge additional demands of a guestworker program onto an already overwhelmed and confused bureaucracy would be massive fraud."

Mark Krikorian

Mark Krikorian is the executive director of the Center for Immigration Studies. In this article Krikorian argues against a guest worker program, which he claims would overwhelm Homeland Security and lead to even more illegal immigration. Instead, Krikorian wants the government to enforce already existing immigration laws.

AS YOU READ, CONSIDER THE FOLLOWING QUESTIONS:

1. According to Krikorian, how is illegal immigration linked to terrorist activity?

Mark Krikorian, "Borderline Insanity," *The National Interest*, vol. 79, Spring, 2005, p. 70–72. Copyright © *The National Interest* 2005, Washington, D.C. Reproduced by permission.

2. What two assumptions about guest worker programs are false, according to the author?
3. What does Krikorian say causes networking to create more immigration, which then creates even more immigration, both legal and illegal?

President Bush has pledged to expend political capital to pass an immigration plan that would legalize illegal aliens currently in the United States as "temporary workers" and import an unlimited number of new workers from abroad—something he reiterated in his State of the Union address. One of his principal arguments has been that such an initiative would enhance America's security by allowing enforcement authorities to focus their efforts more narrowly, by shrinking the haystack that the terrorist needles are hiding in. To use a different analogy, a guestworker or amnesty program would deny terrorists cover by draining the pool of ten million illegal aliens and ensure that an ongoing flow of foreign workers comes through legal channels.

On the surface, this appears reasonable. Terrorists have indeed benefited from our lawless immigration system. A 2002 study by the Center for Immigration Studies found that the 48 Al-Qaeda–affiliated operatives in the United States from 1993 to 2001 had compromised virtually every facet of the immigration system. Mass illegal immigration creates a large market for fraudulent documents, allowing the 9/11 hijackers, for instance, to amass more than sixty U.S. driver licenses. Mass illegal immigration also overwhelms the resources available to law enforcement, creating the conditions whereby Gazi Ibrahim Abu Mezer, a Palestinian who was part of the 1997 conspiracy to bomb the subway in Brooklyn, was actually caught by the Border Patrol but was released into the United States on his own recognizance because of inadequate detention space. . . .

The System Is Overwhelmed

Shrinking the number of illegal aliens living in the United States, reducing the flow of new illegals and generally restoring order to our anarchic immigration system are clearly security imperatives. But can a guestworker program achieve these goals? It cannot. Support for such an approach is premised on two basic assumptions that turn out to be false.

The first assumption is that the Department of Homeland Security has the administrative capacity to properly screen and track millions of currently illegal aliens and millions more new foreign workers. Such an assertion is laughable to anyone with even a passing familiarity with our immigration bureaucracy. Even before 9/11, the old Immigration and Naturalization Service was choking on mass immigration. Last year, Eduardo Aguirre, head of the new agency that handles immigration services, told Congress:

Illegal border crossings continue as the U.S. government debates the best way to address the problem.

In any typical work day, our workforce of 15,500 (one-third of whom are contractors) will: process 140,000 national security background checks; receive 100,000 web hits; take 50,000 calls at our Customer Service Centers; adjudicate 30,000 applications for immigration benefits; see 25,000 visitors at 92 field offices; issue 20,000 green cards; and capture 8,000 sets of fingerprints and digital photos at 130 Application Support Centers.

And despite this effort there is still a backlog of four million immigration applications of various kinds. . . .

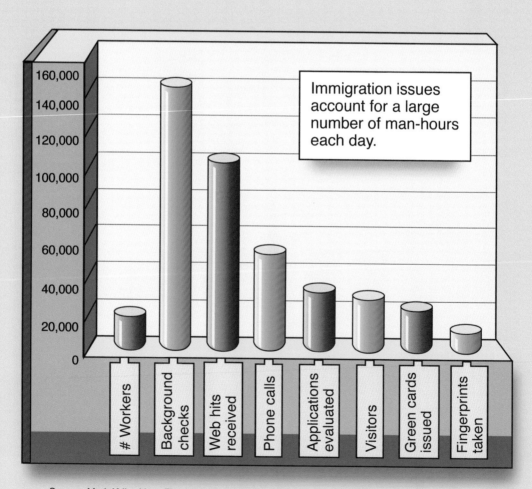

Typical Work Day for Immigration Services

Immigration issues account for a large number of man-hours each day.

160,000
140,000
120,000
100,000
80,000
60,000
40,000
20,000
0

Workers · Background checks · Web hits received · Phone calls · Applications evaluated · Visitors · Green cards issued · Fingerprints taken

Source: Mark Krikorkian, *The National Interest*, 2005.

The result of placing the huge additional demands of a guest-worker program onto an already overwhelmed and confused bureaucracy would be massive fraud. During the last large-scale amnesty for illegal aliens, passed by Congress in 1986 as part of the Immigration Reform and Control Act (IRCA), the number of illegals was smaller than today, and the INS was not undergoing any kind of massive reorganization. But there were still several hundred thousand people who were improperly legalized. Applicants claiming to have been farmworkers described harvesting purple cotton, digging cherries out of the ground and using ladders to pick strawberries. . . .

FAST FACT

The Immigration and Reform and Control Act of 1986 offered general amnesty to many illegal immigrants.

Illegal Immigration Will Continue

The second claim of those promoting a guestworker program as a security measure is that it will end—or at least radically curtail—illegal immigration. Tamar Jacoby, a high-profile spokesperson for the president's plan, recently instructed: "Think of it as a reservoir or a river we're trying to channel into a pipeline. The problem isn't the flow: We need the water. The problem is that the pipeline isn't big enough." In other words, there is a fixed amount of foreign labor that the American economy demands, and our immigration arrangements accommodate only a portion of that demand, forcing the rest to come in illegally. If only the illegal overflow were legalized, the problem would disappear.

Immigration, however, is very different from what this image suggests. The labor market is not designed for any specific level of immigration, or even a specific number of unskilled jobs. It is not a static system, but rather a dynamic one that responds to price signals and substitutes factors of production when appropriate. Labor is substituted for capital when the price of labor falls (say, through massive importation of foreign workers), and the opposite happens when the price of unskilled labor rises (say, through consistent immigration enforcement). Of course, this is cold comfort to those employers who have relied on the expectation of continued non-enforcement of the immigration law, and they can be expected to fight efforts to restrict the flow of foreign labor. But this is a political problem, not an economic one. The economy would adjust quite easily to a smaller supply of immigrant labor, and the accompanying disruptions would dissipate in short order.

In fact, not only would the guestworker approach not end illegal immigration, it would almost certainly increase it. The largest flow of illegal immigration in our history before the current wave came during the bracero program, which imported Mexican guestworkers during the 1950s and early 1960s. A similar thing happened after the IRCA amnesty of 1986. This shouldn't be a surprise. Immigration always creates more immigration, whether legal or illegal, because it is driven not simply (or even principally) by wage differences but rather by networks—the family and other connections that prospective migrants use to decide where to settle or whether to move at all. Once illegal aliens are anchored here by legal status, and once new workers arrive from abroad, millions of additional people worldwide suddenly will have a connection in the United States, making immigration here a realistic option, independent of their qualification under whatever new rules we impose.

Enforce the Law to Solve the Problem

What, then, would a security-conscious immigration policy look like? A long menu of changes is available, but the first imperative is a commitment to enforce the law. Immigration expansionists routinely claim that our attempts at enforcement have failed, pointing to their preferred policies as more realistic and enforceable. But there has never been any serious, sustained effort to enforce the immigration law. In fact, enforcement attempts by immigration agents are routinely discontinued because of political pressure, with the officials responsible sometimes reprimanded or forced into retirement.

The most responsible approach the president could take toward immigration would be to state unequivocally that the immigration law, whatever it may be, will be enforced across the board, and that those involved in its implementation will no longer be expected to cut corners and look the other way. The result would not be a magical elimination of the illegal immigration problem, but rather a sustained reduction through attrition, as fewer prospective illegals make the trip and more of those already here give up and deport themselves. In this way terrorists would be kept off-balance, their conspiracies interrupted, their sources of cover reduced. A massive amnesty and guestworker program would do the opposite, serving only the interests of our enemies.

EVALUATING THE AUTHOR'S ARGUMENT:

Krikorian argues that guest worker programs would be ineffective because immigration is market driven. Examine his evidence about the economics of immigrant labor usage. Is his evidence compelling or would you need additional data to support Krikorian's argument?

A Guest Worker Program Would Provide Economic Benefits for the United States

"The current system for hiring and admitting foreign workers is complex and burdensome for both the employer and employee."

Elaine Chao

Elaine Chao is secretary of the U.S. Department of Labor. In her congressional testimony, Chao explains that the new guest worker program will provide economic stability for immigrants and a stable workforce for employers.

AS YOU READ, CONSIDER THE FOLLOWING QUESTIONS:

1. What are the five principles that Chao argues should guide immigration reform?
2. What are the benefits of a temporary worker program, according to Chao?
3. Who does Chao say would manage the new guest worker program?

Elaine Chao, congressional testimony before the Senate Judiciary Committee, October 18, 2005. www.aila.org/content/default.aspx?docid=19952.

The effectiveness of border security and interior enforcement initiatives is tied to creating a legal avenue for the workers our economy needs to keep growing. This will allow U.S. enforcement to focus on achieving control of our borders. When integrated with a workable and enforceable temporary worker program, U.S. border security and enforcement resources can be maximized to strengthen our homeland security, stop illegal immigration, and meet U.S. needs for a legal workforce.

The President's Proposal

Last year, the President proposed that we reform our current system for admitting and employing temporary foreign workers in this country. The President set forth principles that should guide comprehensive immigration reform. Those principles are:

- Protect the Homeland by Controlling Our Borders: A new program must support ongoing efforts to enhance homeland security.
- Serve America's Economy by Matching a Willing Worker with a Willing Employer: When no U.S. worker is available and willing to take a job, the program should provide workers for American employers. The process should be as clear, streamlined, and efficient as possible so people can find jobs and employers can find workers in a timely manner.
- Protect the Rights of Legal Immigrants: The program should not permit illegal immigrants to gain an advantage over those who have followed the rules.
- Provide Incentives for Return to Home Country: The program will require the return of temporary workers to their home country after their period of work has concluded.
- Promote Compassion: The program should afford illegal immigrants who are currently working an opportunity to join the temporary worker program and avoid exploitation. Participants in a new program would be able to travel back and forth between their home and the U.S. without fear of being denied reentry into America.

A reformed temporary worker program based on these basic principles will provide America with several benefits, including:

President Bush's proposal suggests that it would benefit the country to match guest workers to jobs when no U.S. citizen is available or willing.

- A More Secure Homeland by Improving the Efficiency and Management of All People Crossing Our Borders: It is in the interest of our country, and each community, to identify foreign visitors and immigrants and clarify the nature of their intentions during their stay.
- A More Prosperous Economy: The program would allow workers to find jobs and employers to find workers, quickly and simply. . . .

A Temporary Worker Program

The President's plan for reform recognizes that foreign workers are drawn to this country because of economic opportunity. These workers find employment here because many important sectors of our economy rely on foreign temporary workers to fill certain jobs when there are shortages of willing and able U.S. workers.

But, the current system for hiring and admitting foreign workers is complex and burdensome for both the employer and employee. The Department of Labor has initiated some regulatory reforms over the past couple of years to help improve procedures in the labor certification process. But making additional effective improvements to our system of admitting and tracking temporary foreign workers will require legislative as well as administrative changes.

The President's plan seeks to address problems in the current temporary worker system by streamlining the process so that willing workers can efficiently be matched with employers who need foreign temporary workers to fill jobs for which there are no willing U.S. workers. The President's plan would also bring illegal immigrants who currently work in an underground economy into the open. And, of course, any reforms that improve the process for workers and employers must be matched with reforms that improve the safety and border security of our country as a whole.

Our current system is overloaded, ineffective at deterring fraud, does not work well for workers or employers, and strains the nation's enforcement abilities. Our country faces a continuing high demand for foreign labor in several sectors of the economy. This demand is strongest among lower skilled occupations and for seasonal positions in businesses and agriculture. This constant, and in many cases increasing, demand for foreign labor strains our current admission system. As the

FAST FACT

Only 46 percent of American voters support a guest worker program, according to a June 2006 *Los Angeles Times* poll.

members of this committee know, some visa programs have annual limits that are often reached in the first few months of the year. This environment creates an unfair system of winners and losers that does not serve our national economic interests. The Department hears

about these problems from employers and from members of Congress. Each year, we receive scores of inquiries from Congressional offices about pending visas or requesting the re-classification of entire groups of workers from one visa category to another with available slots.

Creating a Stable Immigrant Workforce

When the demand for visas overwhelms the supply, many workers resort to illegal border crossings. Once in our country, these workers often use fraudulent documentation in order to obtain employment. As a result, employers can unwittingly hire illegal workers because there is no quick and efficient way to verify the authenticity of identification documents. And of course, some employers knowingly resort to hiring illegal workers because they fail to obtain legal foreign workers or because they do not want to incur the expense of navigating the complex bureaucracy required to obtain a foreign worker with a visa.

A well-designed temporary worker program will help alleviate each of these concerns by providing stability and certainty to workers, employers, and the American people. With a technologically advanced new system in place, workers will have visa documentation that clearly establishes their eligibility to work. Employers will have access to a verification system that enables them to quickly check the eligibility and verify the identity of potential employees. And with increased enforcement efforts, the American public will have confidence that employers are obeying the law and hiring only those people who are in the country legally.

The reforms should enable those who are here unlawfully an opportunity to come forward, apply for a legal temporary work status, and participate in the legal economy. But these people will not be granted amnesty for their violations of law. President Bush strongly opposes amnesty, because it unfairly rewards lawbreaking and because amnesty encourages further illegal immigration. At a minimum, those who come forward will not be offered an automatic pass to citizenship and should be expected to pay a substantial fine or penalty to participate in the temporary program. Applicants for the temporary worker program, including those already in the country, should undergo credentialing procedures and background checks, and at a minimum should have to meet the legal admissibility standards set by Congress. Felons and those in removal proceedings would not be eligible to participate in the program.

Workers should also be issued biometric, tamper-resistant cards that will allow them to cross U.S. borders during their stay here. Currently, many illegal immigrants do not leave the U.S. because it can be costly and dangerous to make a return trip. A new temporary worker program will remedy this situation by providing workers with temporary status the ability to freely travel back and forth to their home country. This will help enable temporary workers to maintain ties to their home and help encourage them to return when their temporary visa expires. . . .

Protection for U.S. Workers

The President is committed to ensuring that every U.S. worker who wants a job can find one. Under the President's plan, U.S. workers come first. U.S. employers would have to make reasonable efforts to find a U.S. worker to fill a job before extending job offers to foreign workers. The temporary worker program must include strong workplace enforcement provisions and incentives for foreign workers to return home when their time in the program is done. These program requirements are necessary to ensure that we protect our jobs for U.S. workers.

The Department of Labor has a limited, but important, role in the current work visa programs. As a prerequisite to hiring a foreign worker through most work visa programs, an employer must first have attempted to hire U.S. workers for the job openings. If that effort proves unsuccessful, an employer may then apply to hire foreign workers with a temporary work visa. The effort by employers to seek out and attempt to hire sufficient numbers of U.S. workers is referred to as a "labor market test."

The Department is responsible for verifying that an employer who wishes to hire temporary foreign labor has properly complied with the labor market test. In addition, the Department is responsible for enforcing the labor standards associated with these temporary worker programs to prevent the exploitation of the temporary workers and guard against adverse employment effects on U.S. workers.

Managing the Program

On the topic of matching willing workers with employers, this Administration believes that the private marketplace, rather than a vast government bureaucracy, is better suited to meet this challenge. The federal government will have a great deal of work to do in completing background checks on temporary worker applicants, issuing visas, and improving border security. Private organizations, whether they are nonprofit or for profit, could help match employers with available workers. Of course, such a system will have to contain some government controls and regulations to prohibit, for example, the imposition of excessive fees on workers. But this Administration fundamentally believes that the private marketplace is best equipped to design and manage an efficient matching system.

The Department of Labor takes very seriously its responsibility to ensure that our workforce, including foreign workers admitted under temporary worker programs, is fully protected by our nation's labor laws. The Department will continue its strong enforcement of labor laws to protect the health, safety, working conditions and pay of all workers. It is this Administration's policy to hold employers accountable and to enforce all labor laws without regard to the legal status of workers. These efforts not only help protect foreign born workers from exploitation, but also help ensure that U.S. workers are not undercut by unscrupulous employers.

EVALUATING THE AUTHOR'S ARGUMENT:

Chao testified that U.S. employers would be required to try to fill all jobs with U.S. citizens before offering the jobs to foreign workers. What are some reasons why this system might not work? What might be done to make the system more effective and ensure that U.S. workers are offered first choice of jobs?

Guest Worker Programs Will Cost the United States Huge Amounts of Money

"Every time people attempt to discuss immigration, they are derided as racists."

Dana Rohrabacher

Dana Rohrabacher is a Republican congressman from California. In this essay Rohrabacher argues that if Congress goes forward with a guest worker program, the cost to the federal government and to federal entitlement programs will be enormous.

AS YOU READ, CONSIDER THE FOLLOWING QUESTIONS:

1. According to Rohrabacher, what are the three things that proponents of open borders want?

2. Rohrabacher warns that the influx of foreign workers will drain one very important government agency and that the elderly should be especially concerned. Which agency concerns him the most?

3. What does Rohrabacher suggest is the solution to prevent a projected financial drain on government entitlements?

Dana Rohrabacher, "Face the Truth," *The American Enterprise*, vol. 16, January/February, 2005, p. 53. Copyright 2005 American Enterprise Institute for Public Policy Research. Reproduced with permission of *The American Enterprise*, a national magazine of Politics, Business, and Culture (TAEmag.com).

The politics of immigration has been a lethal mix in this country. It's a combination of Republicans who capitulate to huge corporate interests wanting to keep wages down, and Democrats who are looking for a new underclass to justify their positions of expanding government programs, which of course gives them political power. Add to this mix the new McCarthyism—every time people attempt to discuss immigration, they are derided as racists. That tactic has harmed the honest debate of an issue vitally important to this country.

Inaccurate Estimates Mislead Congress

The Pollyannas and ostriches who advocate open borders want Congress to believe three things about their pending Social Security agreement with Mexico—all of which are false. First, proponents want us to believe that it will affect only a small number of people. The Social Security Administration claims the agreement will cover only 50,000 Mexicans. The administration came up with that figure by studying the number of Canadian illegal immigrants. The General Accounting Office has noted with remarkable understatement that the Canadian experience is not a good predictor of our immigration realities with Mexico.

> **FAST FACT**
>
> In March 2006 the *New York Times* reported that people supported a guest worker plan provided that workers learn English and pay taxes.

We are talking about huge sums of money—not just for retirement, but for disability payments, premature deaths, caring for the families of illegal immigrants. This is a huge threat to Social Security, and it is an outrageous violation of our obligation to watch out for the senior citizens of the United States. I do not understand why every senior citizen organization in this country is not engaged in this debate. I suspect the answer is that they simply do not realize what is being proposed.

An Increase in Illegal Immigrants Will Result

Supporters of totalization want you to believe that it will not become an inducement to further illegal immigration. I don't know

Estimated Number of People Illegally Present in the United States

Twenty countries—and Mexico—with which the United States has Social Security reciprocity agreements ranked by number of illegal workers

Mexico	4,808,000
South Korea	55,000
Canada	47,000
Chile	17,000
Italy	10,000
France	7,000
Greece	7,000
Spain	7,000
United Kingdom	7,000
Portugal	6,000
Ireland	3,000
Netherlands	3,000
Australia	1,000

Source: US Immigration and Naturalization Service.

whether anyone who makes those claims has taken Economics 101, but the reality is if you pay for something, more of it will be produced. If we spend more money to provide guaranteed lifelong benefits to illegal immigrants, there will be more illegal immigrants. Who in Mexico wouldn't choose to come to America and gain access to U.S. benefits dispensed at U.S. dollar levels, rather than relying on the corrupt and bankrupt retirement system in Mexico?

If Congress passes any kind of illegal immigrant amnesty or guest-worker program, as it has numerous times in the past, every illegal alien who qualifies for amnesty will be qualified for Social Security and will have legal status in the United States. Any of the amnesty or guest-worker programs that we have heard about will mean millions and millions of illegal aliens thrown into the Social Security

Concerns have been raised that a guest worker program would introduce expenses by providing lifelong benefits that could encourage even more immigrants to enter the country illegally.

system just when the baby boomers in this country are retiring. All the time they have worked illegally will be credited to their accounts.

Congress Has an Obligation to U.S. Citizens

America cannot support the whole planet, and Congress has an obligation to look out for our own senior citizens first. This is real: this agreement with Mexico could cost the people we are responsible for taking care of the type of protection and services and resources that they have been promised all of these years by their government.

Congress has one option to stop this insanity. We must pass a law specifically banning work by illegal aliens from qualifying them for Social Security. I have introduced a bill—HR 1631—to prohibit the work histories of non-citizens who are here illegally from being counted toward Social Security earnings. If a bill like this does not pass, a Social Security agreement with Mexico could be a disaster for senior citizens and workers in the United States.

This is not an attack on our friends in Mexico, it's simply a recognition of the fact that they—not American tax-payers—are responsible for watching out for their families and supporting their elderly.

EVALUATING THE AUTHOR'S ARGUMENT:

Rohrabacher argues that financial data from Canadian immigration cannot be applied to the proposed Mexican guest worker immigration program. What evidence does he offer to support this assertion? Do you find his argument convincing? If not, what additional evidence should Rohrabacher have included?

Viewpoint 5

Punishing Employers Will Not Solve the Problem of Illegal Workers

"As a strategy to rein in illegal immigration, crackdowns are mostly myth."

USA Today

In this unattributed editorial the writer argues that past efforts to arrest and charge employers who hire illegal immigrants have not worked, and thus there is little reason to suppose such a plan would work now.

AS YOU READ, CONSIDER THE FOLLOWING QUESTIONS:

1. How many illegal workers were arrested in the government raids on IFCO plants?

2. According to the author, what is the biggest reason why workplace arrests of illegal workers is not effective in curbing hiring of these workers?

3. Why did Operation Vanguard fail, according to the author?

E very few years, when the country goes through one of its paroxysms over immigration, the debate follows a predictable path, reflecting the nation's ambivalence. There are promises to tighten borders, to deal with illegal aliens already here and to crack down on employers who hire and harbor illegal immigrants.

Arrest Employers

It's largely a political charade—the latest installment of which played out Thursday [April 20, 2006], when the Bush administration promised a new enforcement strategy: using criminal statutes against employers who blatantly ignore the law. Homeland Security Secretary Michael Chertoff trotted out Exhibit A: Raids in 26 states at

Encouraging employers to hire only legal immigrants may seem like a good idea, but some fear that it could slow the economy if the illegal workers are cut out of the workforce.

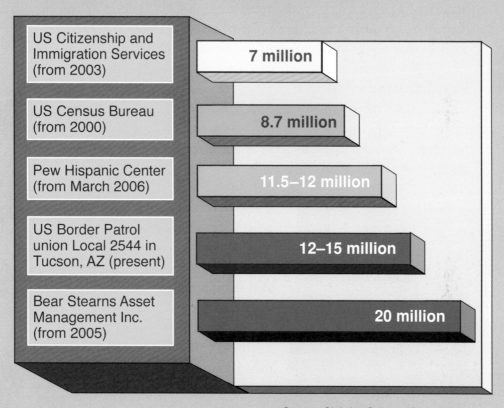

How Many Illegal Immigrants?

Estimates range from as few as 7 million living in the United States to as many as 20 million, depending on who is counting. The figures are part of the debate on immigration reform measures.

US Citizenship and Immigration Services (from 2003)	7 million
US Census Bureau (from 2000)	8.7 million
Pew Hispanic Center (from March 2006)	11.5–12 million
US Border Patrol union Local 2544 in Tucson, AZ (present)	12–15 million
Bear Stearns Asset Management Inc. (from 2005)	20 million

Source: *Christian Science Monitor*, 2006.

the plants of IFCO Systems North America Inc. Not only did the government arrest more than 1,180 illegal workers, it also charged several IFCO managers in a scheme to hire and harbor them.

Fine, as far as it goes. If companies are allowed to flout the law, everyone loses respect for it. But as a strategy to rein in illegal immigration, crackdowns are mostly myth. The law is enforced only in fits and starts. Beginning in the late 1990s, enforcement plummeted.

In 1998, immigration authorities arrested about 14,000 illegal immigrants at worksites. The next year, arrests dropped by 80%—and kept on dropping, according to a study by Congress' non-partisan Government Accountability Office [GAO]. In 2003, there were just 445 arrests, the GAO reported.

Even if the government wanted to use worksite arrests to stamp out illegal immigration, it doesn't have the manpower. Homeland Security has about 325 agents to enforce the law against 7.2 million illegal workers. But the biggest reason crackdowns on business don't work is that powerful forces don't want them to.

Past Efforts Failed

Consider a strategy tried in 1998, one that had all the makings of success. In Operation Vanguard, authorities focused on the meatpacking industry in Nebraska. After comparing records at every plant in the state against Social Security numbers, they notified the employers of about 4,700 suspect workers. The program worked so well that 3,500 workers disappeared.

FAST FACT

According to a June 2006 Gallup poll, 74 percent of individuals surveyed think that illegal immigrants take the jobs that no one wants.

The long-range plan was to repeat the experiment industry by industry and state by state. This, immigration authorities logically concluded, would persuade employers that it's more economical to hire legal workers. With jobs drying up, illegal immigration would slow. All of this would be done without disruptive raids or wholesale deportations, such as those voted by the House of Representatives in January. But the plan worked too well. Unions, immigration advocates, the industry and Nebraska's politicians stampeded to protest. Plants couldn't find workers. Livestock demand dropped. Nebraska's economy was disrupted, and immigrant families were torn apart. In a year, Vanguard was gone.

What to conclude from the experience? First, that the law can be enforced, just as so many people today are urging. But also that once the results appear, many of those same people are likely to change their minds.

That is the perpetual dilemma of America's immigration debate. People want the law to have meaning. They also want the services that the immigrants provide. Ways exist to address that dilemma—expanded legal immigration coupled with meaningful employer enforcement, for instance. But for now, trumped-up schemes and anti-immigrant pandering rule the stage.

EVALUATING THE AUTHOR'S ARGUMENT:

This editorial provides a lot of facts and details and information about past efforts to punish employers for hiring illegal workers. Compare this method of presenting evidence against the argument in the following article. Which argument is more convincing? Would punishing employers help to stop illegal immigration?

Employers Who Hire Illegal Immigrants Should be Punished

"Enforcement with employers will help to dry up the incentive for illegal entry into this country."

Howard Stephenson

Howard Stephenson is president of the Utah Taxpayers Association and a Republican Utah state senator. In this essay Stephenson lays out a plan to offer incentives for legal entry of workers. In addition, Stephenson states that employers must be punished for continuing to hire illegal workers.

AS YOU READ, CONSIDER THE FOLLOWING QUESTIONS:

1. According to Stephenson, how did the United States create the problem of illegal workers?
2. How does Stephenson's incentive plan work?
3. What are "golden handcuffs"?

Howard Stephenson, "Restoring Rule of Law—an Immigration Reform Proposal," *The Enterprise*, May 15–21, 2006. Reproduced by permission.

ongress is currently dealing with the problem of illegal immigration. Or at least those running for re-election are forced to discuss the issue because the American public is confused and concerned. I would like to present in this column my proposal for ending illegal immigration by utilizing the free enterprise system in the enforcement of worker visas. . . .

The United States Created the Problem

The United States government has conflicting immigration laws and economic policies. Congress and the executive branch have put the economic policies calling for cheap labor ahead of the enforcement of immigration laws. They have ensured that the Immigration and Naturalization Service (INS) will look the other way while our porous borders allow the free flow of illegals into the United States.

Employers Should Pay Fines for Hiring Illegal Immigrants

A majority of Americans agree the federal government should enforce present laws for heavy fines for employers who knowingly hire illegal immigrants.

	Total (1,012) %	18–24 (104) %	25–34 (133) %	35–49 (272) %	50–64 (258) %	65+ (213) %
Agree	79	71	83	88	90	79
Strongly	67	40	64	74	74	70
Moderately	12	17	13	12	13	6

Source: *Americans Talk About Illegal Immigration*, RoperASW. Negative Population Growth, March 2003.

The presence of 11 million illegal immigrants is not by accident. They have not forced themselves upon our country without our permission. The United States government has allowed and in some ways encouraged their entry into our country.

A Nation That Cannot Control Its Borders Cannot Prevent Terrorism

While the U.S. economy receives the benefits of cheap labor through lower agricultural and construction prices and less expensive restaurant meals and hotel stays, the trafficking of illegal workers poses serious threats to national security. If we cannot control workers crossing the border, how can we ensure that some who cross the border are not terrorists?

Congress simply must enforce worker visa requirements to ensure that any immigrant workers who are in this country are here legally. To do anything less is to violate our own rule of law and place our national security at risk.

Congress Should Use the Private Sector to Enforce Worker Visas

It is unreasonable to expect the INS to monitor and control 11 million migrant workers and ensure they are legal without the assistance of the free enterprise system. The INS budget simply could not be large enough to do the job without an undue burden on the U.S. taxpayer. The costs of this monitoring and enforcement should be borne by the immigrant workers and their employers rather than being shifted to the American taxpayer.

This monitoring can be accomplished by requiring each worker to post a bond prior to receiving a visa. The bond would require a cash deposit. Instead of paying cash to the "coyote" who currently assists workers in getting across the border illegally, this money would be used to purchase the bond which would also require with-

FAST FACT

According to the Immigration and Reform and Control Act of 1986, employers are required to use official government documentation to verify that workers are legal U.S. citizens.

Immigrants across the country have participated in demonstrations sending the message that they are a force to be reckoned with.

holding a percentage of wages in a trust account held by a third party trust. This trust account would belong to the worker if he complied with the terms of his visa and would be given to him when he returned to his country. It would effectively become "golden handcuffs" that would be a tremendous incentive for good behavior. However, if he violated the terms of his visa or engaged in criminal activity while in the United States, his trust account would be forfeited and if it was not sufficient to pay the total face value of the bond, the remainder would be taken from the pooled trust of other workers, ensuring that all visa holders are interested in their coworkers' compliance with the law and the terms of their visa.

Congress Should Set a Date When Employers Will Be Prosecuted for Hiring Illegal Workers

Strict enforcement requires that employers have birth certificate and social security authentication available to ensure that foreign workers are not producing false documents. Sufficient time should be allowed for employers to ensure that their workers have bonded visas with a time certain set—say, Jan. 1, 2007—after which employers will be prosecuted for hiring illegal workers. This enforcement with employers will help to dry up the incentive for illegal entry into this country. Instead of illegal workers coming across the border in the dark of night, legal workers should come across the border on buses with worker visas in their hands for jobs already determined.

This solution engages the natural incentive of a cash award (an employee receiving the money in his trust account) when the worker complies with the terms of the visa.

It's time Congress begins enforcing the laws of our country instead of looking the other way

EVALUATING THE AUTHOR'S ARGUMENT:

Stephenson argues that the United States has invited illegal workers to come to this country. Is his evidence for this statement convincing? Do the incentives that he suggests offer a solution to the problem?

Facts About Immigration

Illegal Immigration to the United States

- In a June 2006 Gallup poll, only 17 percent of U.S. citizens thought that immigration quotas should be raised to permit more immigrants to enter the United States legally.

- Nearly one out of every ten children born in the United States is the child of an illegal immigrant.

- About 1.7 million people, or one-sixth of the undocumented immigrant population, is under eighteen years of age.

- In November 2006 voters in New Mexico repealed an article in the state constitution that barred illegal immigrants from owning land.

- The 1986 amnesty program allowed an estimated 3.2 million illegal immigrants to become U.S. citizens.

- Of adult illegal immigrants over age twenty-one, 61 percent have not completed high school.

- Nearly 90 percent of Americans surveyed in spring 2006 said they favor a guest worker program that would give more immigrants the opportunity to work in the United States temporarily.

- The unemployment rate for unauthorized workers who arrived between 2000–2005 was estimated to be about 5.8 percent.

- California's Proposition 187, which was passed in 1994, denied schooling and medical care to illegal immigrants.

- A majority of Americans believes that illegal immigrants are taking jobs that Americans do not want.

- In 2006 two-thirds of Americans surveyed said that illegal immigrants should be allowed to keep their jobs and apply for legal status.

- In 2005 nearly five hundred illegal immigrants died trying to cross the border between Mexico and the United States.

- More than 35 percent of undocumented workers arrived in the United States between 2000–2005.
- The construction industry is estimated to be the largest employer of undocumented workers, with an estimated 1.4 million illegal workers.

Legal Immigration to the United States

- In 1892 Immigration and Naturalization Service opened a center at Ellis Island in New York.
- In 1917 the Asian Barred Zone Act denied entry to anyone from an area that included South Asia through Southeast Asia and the islands in the Indian and Pacific Oceans.
- During the colonial period, most immigrants to the United States came from northern Europe.
- Immigrants and their U.S.-born children accounted for 55 percent of the increase in the U.S. population since 1966. Of these immigrants, 29 million were Latino in origin.
- In 2000 the foreign-born population in the United States was 9.5 percent of the total population.
- According to the 2000 census, one-fifth of the U.S. Hispanic population lives in Los Angeles, California.
- The Asian Indian population in the United States doubled between 1996 and 2006 due to the increased demand for high tech workers.
- Immigrants have founded several highly successful high tech businesses, including Sun Microsystems, AST Computer, Computer Associates, and Wang Laboratories.
- More than 70 percent of immigrants are over age eighteen when they arrive.
- Twenty-three states have passed measures that make English the official language.

Immigration Around the World

- The foreign-born population in Australia was 22.7 percent of the total population in 2000, but in Great Britain the foreign-born population was only 3.9 percent.

- It is estimated that more than 240,000 illegal African immigrants enter Europe each year. Most pay about three thousand euros to a trafficking organization to expedite their way.
- Great Britain officials estimate that they stopped thirty thousand people with invalid documents from entering the country in 2004.
- In 2002 more than 696,000 illegal immigrants entered Italy without a residence permit. Three out of every four immigrants living in Italy are there illegally.
- In order to immigrate to any southern European country, immigrants must hold a work permit issued in advance.
- In Spain most illegal immigrants come from urban areas of undeveloped countries with a surplus of educated workers and too few jobs.
- In June 2006 the United Nations reported that there were nearly 200 million migrants living outside their own home countries.
- The BBC reported that at the beginning of 2000, one of every thirty-five people was an international migrant.
- In Canada 21 percent of the workforce is composed of immigrant workers.
- In 2002 Afghanistan had the largest number of refugees flee the country. Of the 10.4 million people with refugee status, more than 2.5 million were from Afghanistan.
- Asian Indian immigrants sent more than $10 billion back to their home country.

Organizations to Contact

The editors have compiled the following list of organizations concerned with the issues debated in this book. The descriptions are derived from materials provided by the organizations. All have publications or information available for interested readers. The list was compiled on the date of publication of the present volume; the information provided here may change. Be aware that many organizations take several weeks or longer to respond to inquiries, so allow as much time as possible.

American Civil Liberties Union (ACLU)
125 Broad St., 18th Floor
New York, NY 10004
Web site: www.aclu.org/safefree/index.html

The ACLU works to extend rights to segments of the U.S. population that have traditionally been denied civil/equal rights, including Native Americans and other people of color, women, people with disabilities, immigrants, and the poor.

The American Immigration Center Incorporated
(800) 814-1555
e-mail: info@us-immigration.com
Web site: www.us-immigration.com

The American Immigration Center Incorporated is a private company that offers self-help immigration and citizenship products. The center publishes and distributes self-help and information products relating to U.S. immigration and citizenship.

The American Immigration Law Foundation
918 F St. NW, 6th Floor
Washington, DC 20004

e-mail: info@ailf.org

Web site: www.ailf.org

The American Immigration Law Foundation is a tax-exempt, not-for-profit educational, charitable organization that is dedicated to increasing public understanding of immigration law and the value of immigration to American society.

Bureau of Democracy, Human Rights, and Labor
U.S. Department of State
2201 C St. NW
Washington, DC 20520
Web site: www.state.gov/g/drl

The Bureau of Democracy, Human Rights, and Labor is the official U.S. agency that is charged with the effort to promote democracy, protect human rights and international religious freedom, and advance labor rights for all people.

Department of Homeland Security
Washington, DC 20528
(202) 282-8000
Web site: www.dhs.gov/ximgtn

The Department of Homeland Security replaced the Immigration and Naturalization Service in 2002. The Department of Homeland Security provides immigration-related services and enforces federal immigration laws. Their stated purpose is to strengthen border security and interior enforcement and reform immigration processes.

Federation for American Immigration Reform
1666 Connecticut Ave. NW, Suite 400
Washington, DC 20009
(202) 328-7004
fax: (202) 387-3447
Web site: www.fairus.org

The Federation for American Immigration Reform (FAIR) is a national, nonprofit, public-interest, membership organization whose members believe that immigration policies must be reformed to serve the national interest. FAIR seeks to improve border security, to stop illegal immigration, and to promote immigration levels consistent with the national interest. FAIR describes itself as a nonpartisan group.

Human Rights Watch
350 Fifth Ave., 34th Floor
New York, NY 10118-3299
(212) 290-4700
fax: (212) 736-1300
e-mail: hrwnyc@hrw.org

Human Rights Watch is an independent, nongovernmental organization, supported by contributions from private individuals and foundations worldwide. Human Rights Watch is the largest human rights organization based in the United States. Human Rights Watch investigates human rights abuses in all regions of the world, publishes information about human rights abuse, and works to correct these abuses.

Immigration History Research Center at the University of Minnesota
Elmer L. Andersen Library
Suite 311, 222 21st Ave. S.
Minneapolis, MN 55455
(612) 625-4800
Web site: www.ihrc.umn.edu/index.php

The Immigration History Research Center is an interdisciplinary research center that focuses on immigration to the United States. The center provides historical and scholarly perspectives for the debate about immigration.

National Immigration Forum
50 F St. NW, Suite 300
Washington, DC 20001
(202) 347-0040
fax: (202) 347-0058
Web site: www.immigrationforum.org

The National Immigration Forum is an immigrant rights organization that is dedicated to upholding the American tradition of welcoming immigrants. The forum works with hundreds of associate organizations and other national groups on immigration policy issues.

National Immigration Law Center
3435 Wilshire Blvd., Suite 2850
Los Angeles, CA 90010
(213) 639-3900
e-mail: info@nilc.org
Web site: www.nilc.org/index.htm

The National Immigration Law Center's goal is to protect the rights of low income immigrants and their family members through the development of in-depth analyses of proposed legislative and regulatory changes.

National Network for Immigrant and Refugee Rights
310 Eighth St., Suite 303
Oakland, CA 94607
(510) 465-1984
fax: (510) 465-1885
e-mail: nnirr@nnirr.org
Web site: www.nnirr.org

The National Network for Immigrant and Refugee Rights (NNIRR) is a national organization. It is composed of local coalitions and immigrant, refugee, community, religious, civil rights, and labor organizations. The purpose is to share information and educate the public about important immigrant and refugee issues.

Pew Hispanic Center
1615 L St. NW, Suite 700
Washington, DC 20036-5610
Web site: www.pewhispanic.org

The Pew Hispanic Center is a nonpartisan research organization supported by the Pew Charitable Trusts. The mission is to improve understanding of the U.S. Hispanic population and to chronicle Latinos' growing impact on the entire nation.

For Further Reading

Books

Bigelow, Bill, *The Line Between Us: Teaching About the Border and Mexican Immigration*. Milwaukee, WI: Rethinking Schools, 2006. In this book, a teacher explains how to teach students about Mexican immigration and what it means to cross the border illegally into the United States.

Buchanan, Patrick J., *State of Emergency: The Third World Invasion and Conquest of America*. New York: Thomas Dunne, 2006. In this book Buchanan warns that the southwest United States is being conquered by Mexico through a torrent of illegal immigration that will transform the United States into a low-wage workforce. He warns that recent immigrants are detached ethnically, linguistically, and culturally from the rest of the U.S. population.

Dudley, William, ed., *Examining Issues Through Political Cartoons: Illegal Immigration*. Farmington Hills, MI: Greenhaven, 2003. The cartoons in this book explore various aspects of the illegal immigration debate, including economics and national security.

Haines, David W., and Karen E. Rosenblum, eds., *Illegal Immigration in America: A Reference Handbook*. Westport, CT: Greenwood, 1999. This is a comprehensive review of the subject that covers all aspects of illegal immigration from a variety of perspectives.

Hansen, Victor Davis, *Mexifornia*. San Francisco: Encounter, 2003. Hansen examines the problems and in some cases benefits that significant Mexican immigration has brought to California.

Hing, Bill Ong, *Deporting Our Souls: Values, Morality, and Immigration Policy*. Cambridge, UK: Cambridge University Press, 2006. In this book the author examines several areas of immigration policy, including undocumented workers, the immigration selection system, deportation of aggravated felons, national security, and immigration policy.

Huntington, Samuel P., *Who Are We? The Challenges to America's National Identity*. New York: Simon & Schuster, 2004. Huntington warns that globalization is the threat to the society that was envisioned by the men who founded the United States. In particular he warns about unlimited immigration from Mexico.

LeMay, Michael, and Mildred Vasan, eds., *Illegal Immigration: A Reference Handbook*. Santa Barbara, CA: ABC-CLIO, 2007. This book provides an overview of the problem of illegal immigration, with information about immigration laws passed since 1965 and proposed solutions.

Ngai, Mae M., *Impossible Subjects: Illegal Aliens and the Making of Modern America*. Princeton, NJ: Princeton University Press, 2004. This book focuses on American public policy and law from 1924 to 1965.

Wucker, Michele, *Lockout: Why America Keeps Getting Immigration Wrong When Our Prosperity Depends on Getting It Right*. New York: Public Affairs, 2006. This book deals with what the author calls America's growing isolationism and argues that immigrants should be able to come here and work legally while businesses that employ and exploit the undocumented should be punished.

Yoshida, Chisato, *Illegal Immigration and Economic Welfare*. Heidelberg, Ger.: Physica-Verlag, 2000. This book explores the problems of illegal immigration, not only for the destination country but for the labor exporting country, since border patrol and employer sanctions affect both economies.

Yoshida, Chisato, and Alan Woodland, *The Economics of Illegal Immigration*. Hampshire, UK: Palgrave, 2005. This book looks at whether current immigration policies are effective in dealing with illegal immigration and includes a discussion of whether sanctions against employers are effective.

Periodicals and Reports

American Legion Magazine, "Immigration Complacency Weakens U.S. Security," September 2004.

Anderson, Stuart, "Impact of Guest Workers on Agriculture," FDCH congressional testimony, January 28, 2004.

Binford, Leigh, "A Generation of Migrants: Why They Leave, Where They End Up," *NACLA Report on the Americas*, July/August 2003.

Camarota, Steven A., *High Cost of Cheap Labor: Illegal Immigration and the Federal Budget*, report, Center for Immigration Studies, 2004.

Carter, Thomas J., "Undocumented Immigration and Host-Country Welfare: Competition Across Segmented Labor Markets," *Journal of Regional Science*, November 2005.

Couch, Jim F., J. Douglas Barrett, and Peter M. Williams, "Total Amnesty for Illegal Aliens?" *World & I*, February 2004.

Custred, Glynn, "Friends and Elites, Chickens and Coyotes," *American Spectator*, November 2005.

Di Rosa, Roger, "Border Security Measures," FDCH congressional testimony, June 17, 2004.

Douthat, Ross, and Jenny Woodson, "The Border," *Atlantic Monthly*, January/February 2006.

Economist, "Americano Dream," July 16, 2005.

First Things, "Immigration Three-Step," March 2006.

Ganley, Elaine, "Costs of Illegal Immigration: Illegals Cost Feds $10 Billion a Year; Amnesty Would Nearly Triple Cost," *America's Intelligence Wire*, August 25, 2004.

Geller, Adam, "Potent Economics of Immigration Could Defy Changes in Law," Associated Press, April 2, 2006.

Goldfarb, Howard, "The Undocumented Worker: Fuller, Holmes, and the Bush Proposal Within Immigration and Labor Law Jurisprudence," *University of Florida Law & Public Policy*, April 2005.

Government Accountability Office, *Immigration Enforcement*, GAO Report to Congressional Requesters, GAO-05-813, August 2005.

Grow, Brian, Adrienne Cater, Roger O. Crockett, and Geri Smith, "Embracing Illegals," *Business Week*, July 18, 2005.

Helman, Scott, "U.S. Rule Remands Proof of Citizenship for Healthcare," *Boston Globe*, April 11, 2006.

Holzer, Harry J., "Testimony on the Impact of Immigration on the Economy," AILA InfoNet Doc. No. 05121565, November 16, 2005. www.aila.org.

Kassabian, David, "Working Immigrants May Help Economy, Experts Say," *La Prensa*, San Diego, November 18, 2005.

Krauthammer, Charles, "First a Wall—Then Amnesty," *Washington Post*, April 7, 2006.

Krikorian, Mark, "Keeping Terror Out: Immigration Policy and Asymmetric Warfare," *National Interest*, Spring 2004.

Meissner, Doris, "Learning from History," *American Prospect*, November 2005.

Moody, John, "Fixating on Security," *Business Mexico*, May 2, 2005.

Nightingale, Demetra Smith, and Michael Fix, "Children of Immigrant Families," *Future of Children*, Summer 2004.

O'Sullivan, John, "The GOP's Immigration Problems—Will the Elites Get a Clue?" *National Review*, September 12, 2005.

Pugh, Tony, "Taxpayers Foot the Bill for Undocumented Immigrants' Medical Care," Knight Ridder Washington Bureau, July 1, 2006.

Reid, William, "Impact of Illegal Immigration," FDCH congressional testimony, November 17, 2005.

Sandler, Michael, "Securing the Borders Just Got Personal," *CQ Weekly*, June 27, 2005.

Searl, Kent, "Immigration Enforcement Is Not in the Realm of Professional Nursing," *Minnesota Nursing Accent*, January/February 2006.

Sharry, Frank, "Immigration Demystified," *American Prospect*, November 2005.

Siciliano, Dan, "Testimony on the Impact of Immigration on the Economy," AILA InfoNet Doc. No. 05121563, November 16, 2005. www.aila.org.

Solomon, Judith, and Andy Schneider, "HHS Guidance Will Exacerbate Problems Caused by New Medicaid Documentation Requirement," Center on Budget and Policy Priorities, June 16, 2006. www.cbpp.org.

Taylor, Stuart, "Hidden America," *Legal Times*, April 10, 2006.

Time, "Inside the Life of the Migrants Next Door," February 6, 2006.

Tyrell, R. Emmett, Jr., "Our Immigration Imbroglio," *American Spectator*, February 2006.

Williams, Dave, "Impact of Immigrants Debated," *Gwinnett Daily Post*, August 16, 2005. www.gwinnettdailypost.com.

Wood, Daniel B., "New Troops at U.S. Border, but the Task Is Vast," *Christian Science Monitor*, July 27, 2006.

Web Sites

Congress and Illegal Immigration (www.congressandimmi gration.com). This Web site provides current information about congressional bills that deal with illegal immigration.

The Heritage Foundation (www.heritage.org/Research/Features/ Issues/issuearea/Immigration.cfm). This Web site is focused on the need to secure U.S. borders and stop illegal immigration. It provides a list of the agendas that the Heritage Foundation thinks would best solve the problem of illegal immigration.

Illegal Immigration: Facts & Myths (www.laldef.org/html/factsand myths.pdf). The Latin American Legal Defense and Education Fund uses this Web site to provide information about the contributions that illegal immigrants provide to the United States.

Immigration: The Demographic and Economic Facts (www. cato.org/pubs/policy_report/pr-imsum.html). This Web site provides many demographic and economic facts about immigration. This is an effort to dispel myths and provide more accurate information about immigration issues.

United States Immigration Support (www.usimmigrationsupport. org). This Web site is not an official government agency site. Instead, this is an independent organization dedicated to helping individuals and their families through the U.S. immigration process. U.S. immigration support provides forms, legal books, and a do-it-yourself immigration guide.

Index

should be punished 106–10

F
Farmer, Pat, 62–63
Feinstein, Dianne, 36

G
Government, local, 52–55, 58–63,
    63–66
Government, U.S.
    costs of illegal immigrants to, 46,
        47–49
    tax payments vs. costs, 20
Guest worker programs. *See*
    Amnesty/guest worker programs

H
Harvard Latino Law Review
    (periodical), 15
Health care workers, 66–68
Hensley, Tom, 33, 34
Hong, Chung-Wha, 14
Hospitals
    in border areas, 24–25, 36–37
    closures of, 65
    collection of patient data by, 66

I
ICE (Immigration and Customs
    Enforcement), 52–55
Illegal immigrants
    average household income of, 15
    benefit U.S. businesses, 28–34
    costs to hospitals, 24–25
    estimates on, 53, 98, 103
    harm U.S. businesses, 35–39
    have negative impact, 18–27
    have positive impact, 13–17
    industries dependent on, 16,
        33–34

INS apprehensions of, 77
jobs performed by, 16
Mexican, 52
as percent of selected states' total
    population, 30
Illegal immigration
    economic benefits of, 40–49
    guest worker program and
        benefits of, 75-80
        negatives of, 81–87
Illegal Immigration Reform and
    Immigrant Responsibility Act
    (1996), 11, 29
Immigration in U.S. history,
    9–11
Immigration and Customs
    Enforcement (ICE), 52–55
Immigration and Nationality Act
    (1952), 11
Immigration and Naturalization
    Service (INS), 83
    apprehensions of illegal immi-
        grants by, 77
    typical workday for, 84
Immigration laws
    local police should enforce,
        51–55
    in U.S. history, 10–11
Immigration Reform and Control
    Act (IRCA, 1986), 79, 85,
    108
    illegal immigration increased
        following, 86
Immigration system
    attempts at reform of, 63
    Bush's proposed reform of, 76,
        79–80, 82, 89–90
    terrorists benefit from, 82
INS. *See* Immigration and
    Naturalization Service

IRCA. *See* Immigration Reform and Control Act

J
Jacoby, Tamar, 85
Journal of American Physicians and Surgeons, 65

K
Kennedy, Edward, 63
Kice, Virginia, 55
Kobach, Kris, 53

L
Labor Appropriation Act (1924), 10
Lipton, Francine, 15, 16
Los Angeles Times (newspaper), 52

M
Mansoor, Allan, 53, 54, 58
Martini, Robin, 14
Medicare, 45
Medicare Modernization Act, 72
Mezer, Gazi Ibrahim Abu, 82
Morton, Hugh, 31

N
New York Times (newspaper), 97

O
Office of Immigration, 10

P
Papademetriou, Demetrios, 31
Pew Hispanic Center, 31
Police
    border enforcement by, 56–60
    should enforce immigration laws, 51–55

Poulson, Brian, 68–69
Proposition 187 (California), 65

R
Reagan, Ronald, 79
Refugee Act (1953), 11
Reyes, Sarah, 68
Riley, Bob, 52

S
Service industry employees
    should determine residency status, 61–69
    should not determine residency status, 70–73
Social Security
    illegal immigrants contributions to, 15–17
    illegal immigrants benefit, 45
State Criminal Alien Assiatance Program (SCAAP), 24
Surveys
    on employer fines, 107
    on immigrants' commitment to U.S., 21
    on immigration benefits, U.S., 41
    on jobs illegal workers take, 104
    on legal status for illegal immigrants, 14, 15
    on social services for illegal immigrants, 64
    on support for guest worker program, 91

T
The Tax Lawyer (periodical), 15
Taxes, 20, 38
Terrorists/terrorism, 82, 108

U

U.S.-Mexico border, 19
annual deaths of migrants
crossing, 79
enforcement of, 56–60
impact of illegal immigration on
19–21
monitoring of, 42–43
USA Today (newspaper), 59

V

Villaraigosa, Antonio, 55

Visas
better enforcement of, is needed,
108–9
history of, 76, 77–79
quotas on, 91–92
role of Labor Department in, 94
Voegtlin, Gene, 55

W

Wages, 30
Washington Post (newspaper), 14
Woodworth, Mary Kay, 32

Picture Credits

Cover image: Photos.com

AP Images, 12, 16, 23, 32, 37, 42, 48, 50, 54, 58, 67, 72, 74, 78, 83, 90, 99, 102, 109

Maury Aaseng, 14, 30, 38, 46, 53, 64, 77, 84, 98, 103, 107

© 2007, Joseph Paris, BOW Picture Archive, 20